9 8 7 6 5 4 3 2 1
Digit on the right indicates the number of this printing.

ISBN 0-7624-0002-1

Cover, interior, and poster illustrations by Helen I. Driggs
Cover design by Diane Miljat
Interior design by Corinda Cook
Edited by Virginia Mattingly and Gena M. Pearson
Introduction page photograph Museum of Fine Arts, Boston
Poster © 1997 by Running Press

This book may be ordered by mail from the publisher.
Please add $2.50 for postage and handling.
But try your bookstore first!

Running Press Book Publishers
125 South Twenty-second Street
Philadelphia, Pennsylvania 19103-4399

START EXPLORING™

ANCIENT
▲ EGYPT ▲

A FACT-FILLED COLORING BOOK

PETER DER MANUELIAN

ILLUSTRATED BY
HELEN I. DRIGGS

RUNNING PRESS
PHILADELPHIA · LONDON

CONTENTS

▲　▲　▲　▲　▲　▲

III. DAILY LIFE

IV. ARCHITECTURE

V. THE NETHERWORLD

VI. RELIGION

VII. KINGS AND QUEENS

VIII. OTHER FAMOUS EGYPTIANS

IX. SITES

X. DISCOVERIES

XI. EGYPTOLOGY TODAY

▲ ▲ ▲ INTRODUCTION ▲ ▲ ▲

"What has ancient Egypt got to do with me?" That's a good question. After all, here we are at the end of the 20th century, and the earliest Egyptians lived more than 5,000 years ago! What can we learn from the Egyptians?

If you look around, you will find that parts of ancient Egypt are very much alive today. People still wear jewelry with ancient Egyptian designs such as the ankh sign, a symbol of life. Hollywood makes movies such as *Cleopatra*, *The Egyptian*, *The Mummy*, and *Antony and Cleopatra*, which are set fully or partially in ancient Egypt. Pop stars such as Michael Jackson make videos with ancient Egyptian sets and costumes. Composers have written operas with Egyptian themes such as *Aida*.

Our language came from ancient Egypt. Did you know that some English words actually come from the language of Egyptian hieroglyphs? For example, "ebony" comes from the ancient Egyptian *hebny*, with the same meaning. Buildings, too, reflect elements of Egyptian architecture. Where did the idea for the Washington Monument come from? An Egyptian *obelisk!* You can stay in a pyramid-shaped hotel in Las Vegas or enter the Louvre Museum in Paris through a glass pyramid.

When we look at the culture of ancient Egyptians, we find a wonderful world. The following pages will take you on a journey to meet some of these extraordinary people from ancient times. Learn about kings and queens, or the average Egyptian farmer; read some of the ancient Egyptians stories, look at their gigantic buildings, and even find out what they liked to eat for dinner. Though they may have lived 5,000 years ago, the ancient Egyptians are similar in many ways to us today.

Color the pages as you read, and let the pages in turn color your imagination!

A statue of King Mycerinus and his Queen Kha-merer-nebty II from Giza, Valley Temple of Mycerinus.

THE NILE RIVER

WATER OF LIFE

Ｈow many times a day do you use water? What would life be like without it? Water makes life possible. Thousands of years ago, when early bands of travelers came upon the Nile River in northeast Africa, they knew they had found a unique place to live. The Nile begins high in the mountains of Ethiopia, south of Egypt, and cuts through the desert on its way north to the Mediterranean Sea. (This is unlike most of the world's great rivers, which flow from north to south!) In ancient times, this mighty river provided water for drinking, cooking, and washing; fish for eating; a passageway for speedy transportation by boat; flowers for decoration and papyrus plants for making paper. The Egyptians worshiped the force of the Nile in their religion; and later, in the 5th century B.C., a Greek historian named Herodotus (Hair-ODD-o-tus) described Egypt as the "gift of the Nile."

Each year the rainy season came in the Ethiopian highlands and the waters of the Nile rose, laying plenty of fresh, new soil on the ground for the farmers to cultivate. This wonderful environment allowed for several seasons of crops a year in Egypt, although there were years with dangerous floods. Today, Egyptians use modern dams to control the flooding of the river and chemical fertilizers to improve their farming.

The Nile also helped Egyptians to organize their land into two halves: the east (where the sun rises) came to stand for the joys of living each new day, and the west (where the sun sets) became the land where tombs were built and the dead were buried. The only area that was different in shape from the narrow Nile Valley was the Delta, the region of northern Egypt where the Nile splits into two large branches and many small ones that fan out on their way to the Mediterranean Sea.

Floods from the Nile River left behind plenty of fresh, new soil for farming.

THE DESERT AND
THE OASES
LAND OF EXTREMES

Egypt is a very big country, but most of its people have always lived within a very small area along the banks of the Nile River. There the Nile has cool water, fertile soil, shady trees, and lush crops.

Away from the river's edge, the country is mostly desert. As you travel away from the Nile, the plush earth suddenly turns to yellow sand. The air is drier, the sun feels hotter, and you might think you have entered another country. At a point you can even stand with your right foot in the soil of a farmer's field, and your left foot in the sands of the desert! As you move even farther away from the river, you reach the edge of the Nile Valley, where there are rocks and cliffs made of limestone, sandstone, and granite.

Because the desert is so dry and could not support much life, the ancient Egyptians decided to build their burial tombs there. The hot, dry climate helped preserve countless objects—mummies, chairs and tables, pottery, clothing—in tombs built thousands of years ago. Many of these objects are now in museums around the world; others are still buried, waiting to be discovered! The desert also helped protect Egypt against enemies, because it was difficult to invade the country across all that hot sand.

The only places for refreshment away from the Nile River were at the oases. An oasis is a lush place in the desert with underground water sources, where travelers stopped to rest. Egypt has several oases located far out in the western desert. These made it possible for travelers to survive long journeys away from home. In ancient times, many Egyptians lived at the oases year round; archaeologists today have discovered some of their houses, temples, and hieroglyphic inscriptions.

Oases made it possible for travelers to survive long treks through the desert.

EGYPT'S NEIGHBORS
OVERSTEPPING THE BOUNDARIES

The Egyptians believed that they lived in the very best country in the world. They felt that their customs and beliefs came straight from the gods of ancient times and that no other people were so lucky or so blessed. One of the worst things that an Egyptian could imagine was to be alone in a foreign country where things were done differently and to die there, without family or friends.

Part of the reason for this thinking was that, at the beginning of their history (3500–2500 B.C.), the Egyptians did not know much about the countries around them. In fact, their world included only some of the countries directly surrounding them—south of Egypt, ancient Nubia, today called the Sudan; and, further south, the region that is now Ethiopia. To the west of Egypt was the large desert country of Libya. To the east was the Red Sea, Sinai Desert, and, beyond that, the peoples of Sumer, Assyria, Babylonia, Mitanni, Khatti, Israel, and other lands. Today, these countries are known as Iraq, Iran, Jordan, Syria, Israel, Turkey, and Saudi Arabia. To the north was the large Mediterranean Sea, and the cultures of Crete and Greece.

As time passed, though, more and more people traveled among countries, and there were even battles and invasions in which some countries conquered others. At these times, language, fashion, and style were exchanged among people of different countries, and many cultures grew to know each other better.

A) Libya
B) Egypt
C) Sudan
D) Ethopia
E) Somalia

Africa's present regional boundaries

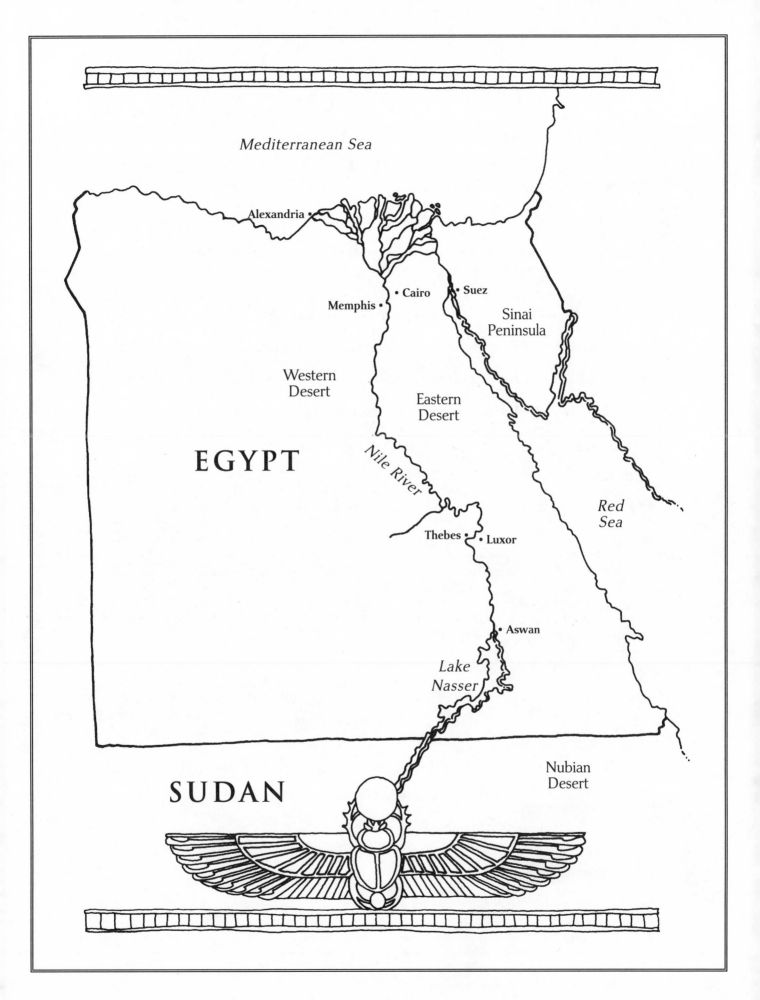

Mediterranean Sea

Alexandria •

• Cairo   • Suez

Memphis •   Sinai
                         Peninsula

Western
Desert   Eastern
                  Desert

EGYPT   Nile River

                              Red
                              Sea

Thebes • • Luxor

                   • Aswan

Lake
Nasser

SUDAN   Nubian
                     Desert

CHILDHOOD
GROWING UP EGYPTIAN

Can you imagine being a kid in ancient Egypt? You would have had lots of sunshine and plenty of room to play outdoors with your friends. Perhaps there was a small pool and garden by your house, where blue and white lotus flowers grew and trees provided welcome shade from the sweltering heat.

As a very young child in ancient Egypt, you would be allowed to run about naked. Later, around age 10, you would wear a loincloth or a simple dress and perhaps grow a lock of hair long on one side of your head (apparently a symbol of youth). If your family had some fields, you would help with the sowing, planting, and harvesting of the crops. Each year, after the Nile flood waters receded, you would watch the adults argue over where the boundaries of their fields used to be!

Most children in ancient Egypt did not go to school. Boys often learned a trade at home from their fathers. Only boys in upper-class families were sent to school to learn to read and write. Their school supplies were a reed pen and clay tablets or flakes of limestone on which to write. If you learned your hieroglyphs well, you might later earn a place in the administration of the town as a scribe or tax gatherer.

As a girl, you probably stayed at home, helping your mother with the chores around the house. There was bread to bake, crops to gather, water from the river or the local canal to collect, and clothing to wash. You might also learn to read and write, and later work in the temple as a songstress, a woman who sang and played musical instruments during religious festivals. Or you could be a priestess of a particular god or goddess. That meant you could manage the crops that were grown, and used for sacrifices to the gods.

Girls often helped their mothers with chores like collecting water from the river.

CAREERS
POWER OF EDUCATION

Do you want to follow a certain career when you grow up? Do you ever change your mind? Do your friends like your idea, or do they suggest something different? It's not always easy to decide what to do in life; while everyone has an opinion, yours is the one that counts the most.

In ancient Egypt, there were many opinions about choosing careers, too. Some of them were written down, and others were not. Most farmers probably wanted their sons to stay on the farm and help with the crops instead of going away to fight a battle. But most of the farmers couldn't read or write, so we don't have many records of their opinions. We do, however, have records of the scribes, the educated people in charge of all kinds of administrative tasks. They collected the taxes, wrote accounts, drafted legal documents, and recorded business transactions. They felt they were in a position of power because they were literate, while so many ancient Egyptians were not. In one famous papyrus, a wise man instructs his apprentice. Here is some of his wisdom:

> **Set your sight on being a scribe; a fine profession that suits you. You call for one; a thousand answer you. You walk freely upon the road. You will not be like a hired ox. You are in front of others . . . come let me tell you the woes of a soldier . . . he dies on the edge of the desert, and there is none to perpetuate his name. . . . Be a scribe and be spared from soldiering!**

It seems the ancient Egyptians knew the value of a good education. Other Egyptian jobs included craftsmen and artisans.

Scribes recorded details of business transactions.

ART
A MATTER OF PERSPECTIVE

Do you know any artists? They usually have something very personal they want to express, and they might use special materials, colors, or words in a way that no one else has used them before.

In ancient Egypt, being an artist was not like this at all. Ancient Egyptian artists performed a community service. You might think of them more as our modern sign painters or wallpaper designers. There was never a lack of work. Tomb walls needed certain scenes and hieroglyphic inscriptions drawn and carved on them. According to ancient Egyptians, all of these things were important because the dead needed them for a successful life in the next world.

Today, some artists try to show a "realistic" view of objects in their work—objects up close look large, and objects far away look small. This is called "perspective." Egyptian artists, though, did not use this approach. Their job was to show everything from the best possible viewpoint. Sometimes this meant combining several different views of the same object. Imagine looking at a tray of coins from the side—you wouldn't see much. An ancient Egyptian artist would paint the tray so that you could see the coins lying on it, as if it were on the floor and you were looking straight down on it. Other parts of the painting, though, would be painted from different angles. This is why Egyptian figures sometimes look strange to us; they show the face from the side, but the eye straight on; the arms from the side, but the chest straight on; and so on. The ancient artists did this by choice, not because they were unable to paint as artists do today. Once you get used to looking at Egyptian figures this way, they won't look strange at all.

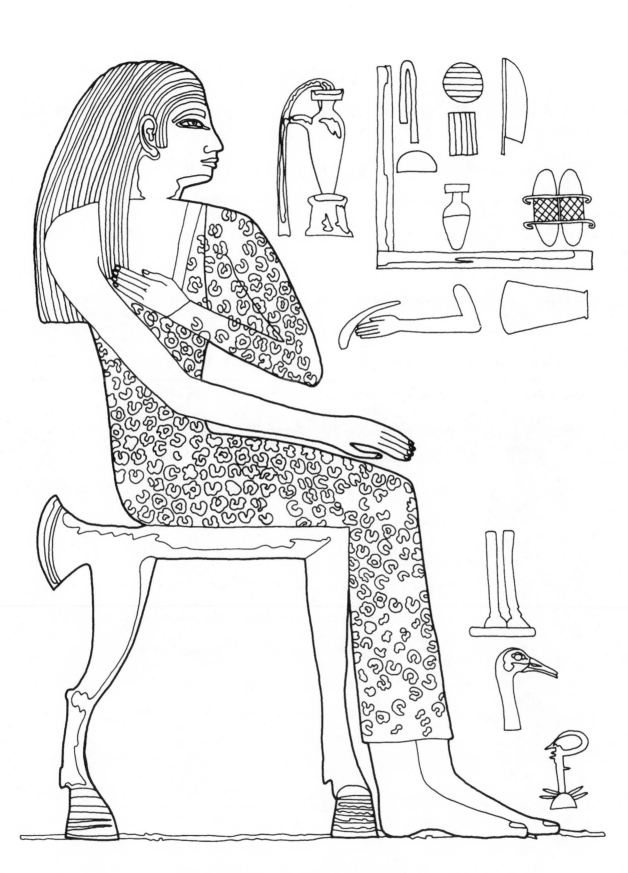

A relief of a seated woman from a stela found at Giza.

MATH AND MACHINES
TECHNOLOGICAL WIZARDS

The Egyptians were among the earliest people to develop technology that helped them in their daily tasks. The Great Pyramid at Giza, built by King Khufu [(KOO-foo) 2606–2583 B.C.], was measured so precisely that the length of one side differs from the other by only a few inches (about 755 feet on the north, and 756 feet on the south). They used rulers and used a measuring unit called a cubit (about the distance from your elbow to the tips of your fingers). They even had simple fractions such as 1/2 and 1/4.

Archaeologists have discovered ancient texts written in ink on papyrus, a form of paper, that have mathematical test questions for students, not so different from those you see in school today. There were also tools like our modern line levels and plumb bobs that used weights, water, rods, and string to tell if an object was perfectly vertical (at a 90° angle) or level with another object.

The banks of the Nile River were sometimes high above the water's edge, too high for people to reach the water. So the Egyptians invented a *shaduf*, a modern Arabic word referring to a kind of lever or machine with a long pole attached to a base that had a bucket on one end and a weight on the other. They lowered the bucket down to the river to fill it with water; then the weight at the other end would pull it back up to the people standing on the river bank. (Imagine a giraffe bending its long neck down to take a drink and then raising it up again.)

Egyptians invented the shaduf to collect water from the high banks of the Nile River.

PAPYRI AND OSTRACA

EARLY PAPER

When you write a letter or draw a picture, you probably use a notepad, stationery, or a sketchbook. Well, in ancient Egypt there was no "paper." But they did write on other materials. The most expensive was papyrus, which was made from long-stemmed papyrus plants that grew along the banks of the Nile. The Egyptians cut the stems into long strips, then wove them together and flattened them. When the papyrus dried, it was polished until it produced a smooth writing surface. If you hold a piece of papyrus up to the light, you can see the crisscross lines of the stems.

The Egyptians wrote with a reed pen and ink made from carbon or finely ground pigments mixed with gum and water. They wrote letters, accounts, legal texts, and religious spells, such as the "Book of the Dead," which Egyptians believed guides the deceased through the afterlife. They wrote poetry, made lists, and even recorded the proceedings of the court trials of tomb robbers. Sometimes they used the papyrus twice, writing on both the front and the back.

For certain projects, the Egyptians didn't want to use up their precious sheets of papyrus, so they wrote on one of the many flakes of white limestone or broken pottery lying on the ground, which we call *ostraca*. Archaeologists have discovered *ostraca* with practice drawings of figures by artists as they prepared to decorate tomb walls, and even parts of famous stories and fables written by schoolboys practicing their letters.

The papyrus plant was used to make paper.

LANGUAGES OF ANCIENT EGYPT
SYMBOLIC CODES

People speak hundreds of languages around the world. Many of these languages have a long history, surviving for hundreds of years. Others were forgotten, then rediscovered and studied by scholars to make sense of them again. Can you imagine how exciting it is to crack the code of a secret message? This is what happened with hieroglyphs, the written language of the ancient Egyptians. The last recorded hieroglyphic inscription dates to A.D. 394. At that point the language was used by only a few Egyptian priests. By that time the majority of Egyptians spoke and wrote in Coptic, Greek, and other languages.

Soon after, the meanings of the signs were forgotten altogether. In the centuries that followed, people believed the hieroglyphic signs were merely magical symbols that did not make up a language anyone could speak. This was the accepted belief for many years, until an incredible discovery in the late 18th century.

▲ The Rosetta Stone ▲

In 1799, in the city of Rosetta near Alexandria, one of Napoleon Bonaparte's soldiers found a granite stone inscribed with the same text in three different languages: Greek and two different forms of ancient Egyptian—hieroglyphs and demotic, the everyday script of the Late Period Egyptians.

The Greek text of the Rosetta Stone was easy to read because people remembered Greek, but the Egyptian texts, belonging to a dead language, were still a mystery.

Later, in 1822, a brilliant French scholar named Jean-François Champollion found the royal names of Cleopatra (Clee-O-patra) and Ptolemy (Tol-me) in both the Greek and the hieroglyphic text. Soon he was able to read the Egyptian alphabet, and the hieroglyphic code was cracked! Thousands of ancient voices that were silent could speak again and be understood. This event marked the birth of the modern field of Egyptology.

A wall relief at Karnak inscribed for King Sesostris I.

HIEROGLYPHIC WRITING
DIFFERENT FORMS

Think of all the different ways you use writing: notes to your friends, stories, schoolwork. You might print carefully, use all capital letters, or even write in cursive.

These different styles of writing are found in ancient Egyptian artifacts, too. Hieroglyphs appear on tomb and temple walls, statues, papyrus, and even jewelry. For quick, informal writing, the Egyptians had a script, derived from hieroglyphs, which we call hieratic. They wrote in hieratic for lists, accounts, and personal letters—though sometimes it is hard even for specialists to recognize the birds, men, and other hieroglyphic signs in the short strokes of the pen.

The Egyptian language changed over the three thousand years it was in use. These different phases are called Old Egyptian, Middle Egyptian, and Late Egyptian. Later, the grammar changed again into a language we call Demotic. Finally, the Egyptian language changed again when Christianity came to the country. Then Greek letters, instead of hieroglyphs, were used. This last stage of ancient Egyptian language is called Coptic and is still used in the Coptic (Egyptian Christian) church today. In daily life, the modern Egyptians speak Arabic.

Some of the hieroglyphic signs could be spoken, while others were written. On paper, though, hieroglyphs were often accompanied by additional symbols or images to help clarify their meaning. For example, to write the word "cat," you might write a hieroglyphic "c," "a," and "t," then show a picture of a cat at the end of the word.

Hieroglyphic writing is one of the most beautiful systems ever created. Texts can be read left to right, right to left, or up and down, depending on which way the signs face. The spacing of the signs is carefully balanced to look even and well organized.

Can you draw hieroglyphs as beautifully as the ancient Egyptians?

A wall relief at Karnak inscribed for King Sesostris I.

Anubis leading the dead to judgment in a scene from the "Book of the Dead."

MUSIC
ANCIENT RHYTHMS

Music was very important to the ancient Egyptians. Every festival, religious ceremony, or party included music. Archaeologists found hundreds of musical instruments perfectly preserved by the dry desert sands. Many of them show the wear from fingers that played them for hours thousands of years ago, while many listeners smiled.

Although their system of writing in hieroglyphs was well developed, the Egyptians did not seem to have a similar system for musical notation. As a result, we can't read or play any ancient Egyptian music today. The instruments have fallen silent. However, we do have many carved and painted scenes showing small orchestras performing, so we can imagine how exciting an Egyptian musical performance was. Perhaps the sounds were not so different from those we hear at weddings and other special events in Egyptian communities today.

Many of our modern instruments evolved from the ones found in ancient Egypt: harps, lutes, lyres, flutes, clarinets, oboes, drums, trumpets, tambourines, and castinets have ancestors from ancient Egypt. The instruments were played by both male and female performers. Often a troop of female players is pictured performing during a party or a male harper (frequently shown as a blind man) is depicted playing for the children of the house by a tranquil lotus pool in a nobleman's garden.

Many modern instruments such as the flute evolved from examples found in Egypt.

LITERATURE
ROYAL PROPAGANDA

Sometimes it is difficult to know the point of the story in ancient Egyptian literature. This is because the Egyptians refer to all kinds of things that we may or may not understand. After all, if you wrote a story about a television, a refrigerator, and a jumbo jet, an ancient Egyptian would not know what you were talking about either! So when we read Egyptian stories, they might have many different meanings. They might be moral tales, to teach us how to live a good and humble life. They might have some political propaganda in them, which means someone wants you to believe in the goodness or the justice of certain characters (usually the king). Or perhaps the story is pure entertainment, with no hidden purpose at all.

King Khufu and the Magicians

One story, written on a papyrus that's now in the Egyptian Museum in Berlin, tells how King Khufu, the builder of the Great Pyramid, sits and listens to stories told by his sons. Each son relates a tale of some magical event in the past. Prince Bau-ef-re tells of Khufu's father, King Snefru, who was bored one day. His chief priest, Dja-dja-em-ankh suggests that Snefru gather lots of beautiful girls and have them row him around his palace lake. This proves to be fun for the king, until one of the girls loses her turquoise pendant in the water and all the girls stop rowing. The King calls for Dja-dja-em-ankh who (long before the story of Moses and the Red Sea) parts the waters and finds the pendant lying at the bottom of the lake.

Then Prince Hor-djed-ef, the King's other son, asks Khufu's permission to bring in a living sorcerer, or magician. This man, named Djedi, makes a goose's head reattach to its body. He also predicts the birth of three children who are to become the first three kings in the next (Fifth) dynasty. This story may be an example of royal propaganda, meant to praise the new family of Fifth Dynasty kings and mark the end of the Fourth Dynasty.

Beautiful Egyptian girls row King Snefru around the palace lake.

AGRICULTURE
AND FOOD
RICH SOILS

Thanks to the powerful Nile River and its annual flooding, there was plenty of rich soil for growing all sorts of crops in ancient Egypt. In fact, most of the population was involved in agriculture, while a much smaller group of people served in temples and ran the government.

To bring water to the fields, the Egyptians developed a series of canals that were far away from the banks of the Nile River. Wheat and barley were the most important grains they grew. Some of the products that were made from them included bread and beer. Did you know the Egyptians were among the world's earliest beer drinkers? For vegetables, they grew garlic, onions, lettuce, and cucumbers; for fruits they grew figs, raisins, dates, and pomegranates. They also collected honey and milk, and made wine from grapes.

Fish from the Nile were a major source of food for the ancient Egyptians. There are fishing scenes with boats and wide nets carved and painted on hundreds of tomb walls all over the country. In addition, the Egyptians raised cattle and fowl; some tomb-wall scenes show ducks hanging up to dry in the marketplace, or butchers cutting meat.

Food played a very important role in Egyptian religion, too. Priests regularly made offerings of food to the gods and to the dead, placing the items before statues or on offering tables carved with hieroglyphic inscriptions. These offerings included bread, beer, meat, wine, fruits, and vegetables. Sometimes as many as 1,000 servings of each! The Egyptians believed that their offerings were magically eaten by the gods. But the food did not really disappear: the priests would gather the food after the offering and pass it out to the contributors who brought it.

The ancient Egyptians made products such as bread and beer from wheat and barley.

TRANSPORTATION
"CURRENT" TRENDS

What was the best way to travel from the Nile delta in the north by the Mediterranean Sea down to Aswan in the south? By boat! For more than 3,000 years of ancient Egyptian history, thousands of boats of all types sailed up and down the Nile. Today it is still one of the most beautiful trips you can take. You pass by lush fields, stark desert, and imposing cliffs, all changing colors in the afternoon sunlight.

The Nile's current flows from south to north, but the wind blows from north to south. So when you look at a boat scene on a temple or tomb wall, you can tell the direction of travel: if the sail is up, the boat is going south with the wind. If the oarsmen are rowing, the boat is going north with the current.

On their earliest pottery, the Egyptians painted pictures of boats. They had simple, one-man skiffs made of papyrus reeds lashed together. They made larger boats from planks of wood that were often imported from Lebanon because Egypt did not have many large, straight trees for boat-building. There were fishing boats, royal barges, kitchen boats, pleasure yachts, and even transport ships for hauling large blocks of stone for construction. The bows and sterns of Egyptian boats often curved upward to look like papyrus plants bound together, and eyes were typically painted on the outside as protectors. There were teams of oarsmen, sails of colorful linen, and huge steering oars at the stern. Canopies and rooms were reserved for owners.

Funerals often proceeded by boat. One of the greatest ancient ships ever found was discovered beside the Great Pyramid of King Khufu at Giza. It was used during his funeral and then taken apart and buried. Another use for boats occurred on festival days, when the priests carried the sacred statue of the god of their temple out of his/her sanctuary and placed it on a boat for a ceremonial visit to other temples, while crowds cheered along the banks of the Nile.

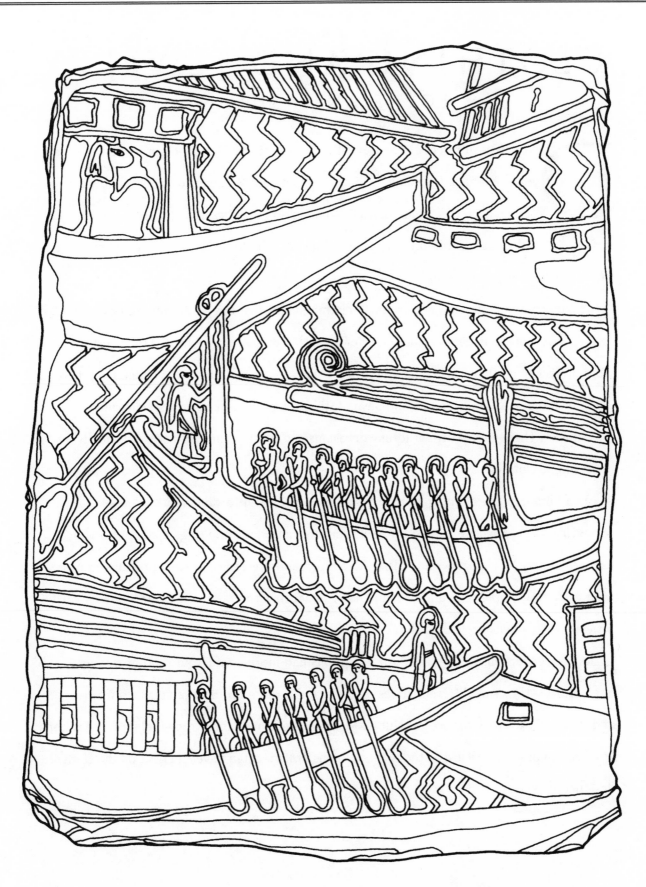

Thousands of boats of all types traveled up and down the mighty Nile River.

CLOTHING AND JEWELRY
EGYPTIAN FASHION

Do you wear different clothes for different occasions? Did the clothes you wore many years ago have the same style as those you are wearing today? Probably not. Well, imagine how many times Egyptian clothing styles changed over 3,000 years! In fact, Egyptologists can often tell the date of a statue by looking at the type of clothing the man or woman is wearing.

Young children often did not wear any clothing in ancient Egypt. But after a few years of age, boys wore a simple loincloth made of linen that was wrapped around the waist. Girls wore dresses that often reached down to their ankles. As young men and women, Egyptians wore linen that could be starched and pleated (folded lengthwise) to make the garments look fancier. These were worn for formal occasions and parties. Farmers and craftsmen wore more simple clothing.

In addition to fine clothing, both men and women of well-to-do families wore a lot of jewelry. Women wore earrings, bracelets, anklets, necklaces, and rings made of floral beads, faience (a shiny blue-glazed material), gold, copper, and precious and semi-precious stones. Men wore rings, bracelets, and broad collars; sometimes the pharaoh rewarded his loyal officials with a necklace called the "gold of honor."

As the generations passed and the Egyptians had more contact with other peoples and cultures, they saw different styles of dress and foreign types of jewelry from Syria and Palestine, Crete, Greece, and Nubia. Many of these new and strange, elaborate fashions affected Egyptian tastes, just as today the fashions of Paris often have an effect on the clothes designed in New York.

Ancient Egyptian women wore elaborate jewelry, clothing, and hairstyles.

FURNITURE
LIVING EGYPTIAN STYLE

You might sit down at a large dinner table with your family in the evenings, but Egyptians did not have such large tables. Everyone had his or her own personal table for eating. However, much of the other furniture from ancient Egypt is very much like the things you have at home. Chairs, stools, beds, chests of drawers, storage boxes—all of these things have been found in excavations along the banks of the Nile.

Archaeologists found little three-legged stools and folding stools they believed were used because they were easy to carry when people traveled, and they did not take up a lot of storage space. In addition to simple furniture, archaeologists have also found tall, elaborately gilded royal chairs, inlaid with wonderful designs and scenes of kings and queens, along with their names in hieroglyphs.

Egyptian beds were also very different from ours. They were quite low, and had footboards instead of headboards. The beds were often slanted, with the head higher than the foot—would you like to sleep like that? Instead of pillows, an Egyptian bed had a headrest, which was a small raised platform that supported your head as you slept. There were also mattresses and blankets made of linen. Archaeologists also found chests and boxes in all shapes and sizes, from the simple to the fancy, as well as latches, knobs, and other locking systems. Some pieces look as if they were made only yesterday!

A headrest from the tomb of King Tutankhamen.

Archaeologists discovered gilded stools inlaid with wonderful designs.

PETS
AN EGYPTIAN'S BEST FRIEND

Who can resist the dreamy-eyed stare of a cat as it stretches out sleepily in a patch of sunshine on the floor? Not the ancient Egyptians; to them pets were friendly companions, hunting helpers, and chasers of mice and insects.

The Egyptians' favorite pet, at least the one shown in Egyptian art most frequently, was the dog. Sometimes they gave their dogs human names and at other times more playful names, such as "Ebony" (after the dog's dark color) or "Grabber." Egyptian men loved to take their dogs with them when hunting for wild game.

Cats were also very important pets. One scene from a New Kingdom tomb shows a cat helping its master catch birds in the marshes. As it leaps into the air, the cat catches one bird in its mouth and another two in each of its front and hind paws. Another scene shows a kitten nestled on the lap of its owner, while the mother cat, wearing a silver earring, looks on from under the chair of the man's wife.

Dogs and cats weren't the only pets loved by the ancient Egyptians. Occasionally, a monkey might be seen frolicking in the garden with the children. Ibexes and gazelles were also among the rarer kinds of pets, and the king might even have his own pet lion. Favorite pets of all kinds were often mummified and buried in tombs to keep their owners company in the afterlife. Sometimes they were even buried in their own little coffins. In the tomb of the high priestess Maat-ka-re, one small mummified figure was first thought to be a baby son or daughter who died young, but recent X-rays showed it was actually a baboon!

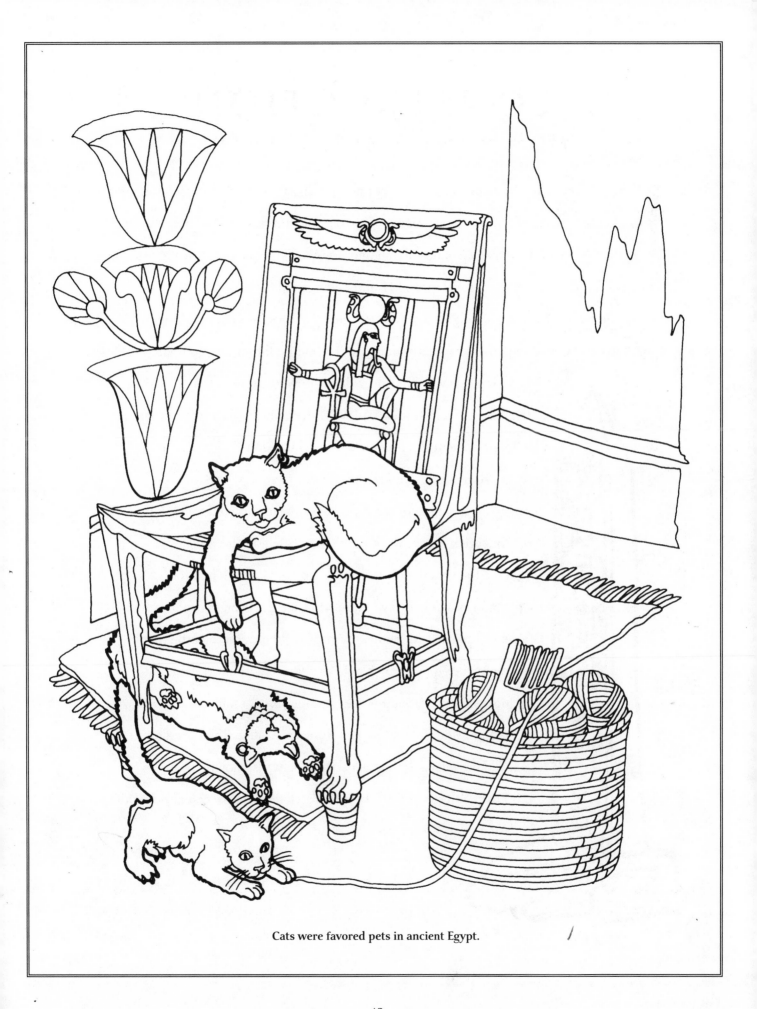

Cats were favored pets in ancient Egypt.

CONSTRUCTION
MONUMENTAL ACHIEVEMENTS

It is a special feeling to walk inside an Egyptian building that is much older than your own house, your town, or even your country. Few other cultures, than that of the ancient Egyptians have left so many wonderful buildings behind: large palaces, private bedrooms, city walls, temples to the gods, royal pyramids, and underground tombs.

While many of these buildings have survived, many others disappeared long ago. Most Egyptians lived in houses made of mudbrick; it is material that does not last for more than fifty years. Many towns and villages developed near the Nile River, and these areas were flooded, plowed over, and rebuilt for centuries. So, many ancient Egyptian towns are buried or no longer exist, but the stone tombs and temples, built farther away from the fields or cut into the cliffs of the Nile Valley, have survived much longer.

Mudbrick houses were simply constructed—the walls were plastered then painted. Wooden beams held up thatched roofs and windows allowed daylight in while air shafts on the roof provided "air conditioning." Monumental stone buildings, on the other hand, were constructed block by block, sometimes with mortar to hold the blocks in place. Scaffolding and mudbrick ramps and debris were raised alongside the building as it became taller. Then the Egyptians removed the ramps as they decorated the walls, moving from top to bottom. You can still see Egyptian styles—plantlike columns, moldings, and cornices—in some buildings today!

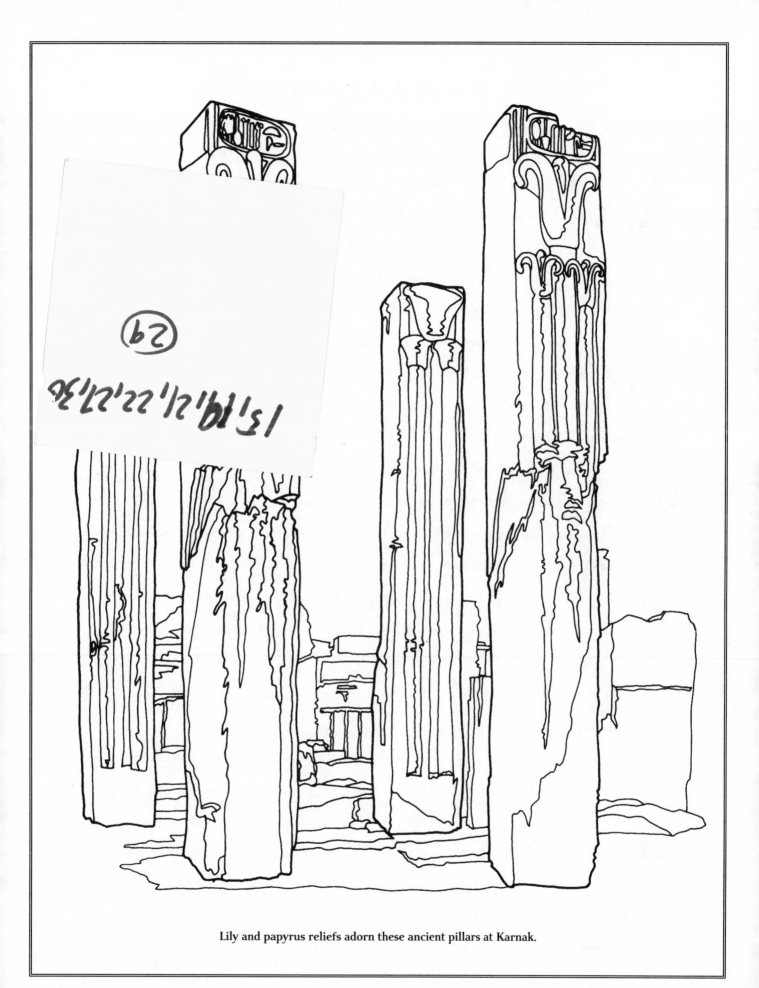

Lily and papyrus reliefs adorn these ancient pillars at Karnak.

PYRAMIDS
GREAT FEATS

When you think of ancient Egypt, you probably think first of pyramids. Did you know that the famous pyramids at Giza [of Kings Khufu, Khafre, (KA-frey) and Menkaure (Men-cow-RAY)] are only three of almost 100 pyramids built in Egypt? And there are even more in Nubia (modern Sudan), which is to the south.

The Great Pyramid was originally 481 feet high. It is almost twice as tall as the Statue of Liberty. The sides are about 756 feet long. The pyramid's rough texture of today is because most of the smooth limestone casing blocks on the outside were removed and used to build the city of Cairo in the Middle Ages. The pyramid is now only 450 feet high.

A pyramid was the tomb of the king, and was believed to be a connecting place between heaven and earth. The Egyptians were great believers in life after death. They believed that they must preserve the body for eternity and put it in a safe place (a tomb) so that the spirit would be able to recognize it and return to it from time to time. The afterlife existence was very similar to "real" life in Egypt.

There were four sides of the pyramid that rose up to the sky, stone by stone, while secret chambers inside held the king's mummy, coffins, and other burial provisions. Each pyramid was really part of a large building complex, with a temple next to it. A long corridor or hallway lead to the river, and to another temple at the end. Smaller pyramids were often built nearby for queens and religious ceremonies.

Many priests worked near a pyramid to make sure the offerings were made to the spirit of the dead king. All around the pyramid, other tombs were built for royal family members and high government officials. This was the pattern of the Old Kingdom (2630–2250 B.C.) and, on a smaller scale, the Middle Kingdom (2061–1784 B.C.), but pharaohs of the New Kingdom (1550-1070 B.C.) chose a very different final resting place (*see Thebes*).

Pyramids were not the product of cruel slave labor. Egyptians believed that creating these tombs for their rulers would help their nation prosper, believing it would bring peace and order.

Ancient Egyptians believed the pyramids were a connecting place between heaven and earth.

TEMPLES
HOUSES OF THE GODS

The Egyptians saw each temple as the sacred place where life began; they had hundreds of such places. The temple was the house of the gods and goddesses whose powers included all the forces of nature. There were gods of the fields and the harvest; a god of the Nile; gods of writing and knowledge, of love, and of protection; and even a goddess of silence!

Some gods were local and others national. Most of the gods had a town or city where they were worshiped in their own temple. The most important temples were built of stone, with a series of courtyards and columns surrounding them. Inside the temple were rooms that became smaller and smaller until you finally reached the Holy of Holies, a room where the statue of the god or goddess was kept. Most people weren't allowed to see this part of the temple. Only the high priests were allowed to take care of the statue by magically feeding it and clothing it every day.

The temple walls were painted with inscriptions praising the gods and depicting different kings making offerings to them. In the New Kingdom, there were great entrance pylons (columns) or gateways leading into the temple, with tall flagpoles and colorful streamers blowing in the wind. Multicolored walls, columns, and hieroglyphs were every-where—a blinding sight in the Egyptian sunshine!

As Egypt became richer and more powerful in the near eastern world the temples also became larger. Hundreds or perhaps even thousands of workers needed to care for them. There were priests, farmers, cleaners, scribes, and musicians, who looked after the temple's affairs. There were even temples built for the continued worship of the pharaoh after his death and burial. Along with pyramids and tombs, Egyptian temples are the most impressive build-ings we have from ancient Egypt.

Luxor Temple has a grand hall lined with enormous columns.

MASTABAS AND ROCK-CUT TOMBS
BURIAL ARRANGEMENTS

In the beginning of pyramid construction only kings were buried in them. Other royal family members and officials were buried in a very different type of building. They were oblong-shaped tombs called mastabas, after the modern Arabic word *mastaba* (bench). Mastabas are solid rectangle or trapezoid shaped structures above the ground with a few rooms inside. Burial shafts lead underground to the main burial chamber where the mummy and coffin were located. Mastabas were sometimes made of mudbrick, but lavish ones were built of limestone.

Images of the deceased and daily life were painted on the walls of the mastabas along with hieroglyphic inscriptions. The Egyptians believed these inscriptions brought prosperity to the dead in the afterlife. A door was also painted on the wall of the tomb. It was believed that this door magically joined the world of the living with the world of the dead. When the priests placed food and other items on the offering table before this decorative door, the spirit of the dead person was thought to come through the false door and eat and drink the offerings.

Other tombs were carved directly into the cliff walls of the Nile Valley. These tombs were found more frequently in the Middle and New Kingdoms. They were perhaps thought easier to hide and protect from tomb robbers who wanted to steal the valuable burial treasure. These walls were also decorated and a shaft contained the actual burial. Thousands of rock-cut tombs still exist today, many in places like Thebes, Aswan, and Amarna. Even the pharaohs of the New Kingdom cut their own tombs into the cliffs because the pyramids were repeatedly robbed.

A statue in the mastaba tomb of Mereruka.

TOMB ROBBERY
PILFERED TREASURE

It is no secret that the ancient Egyptians buried valuable objects with them in their tombs. This is why so many Egyptian tombs were robbed; thieves broke in and stole whatever gold, silver, and precious stones they could carry away. None of the solutions to the tomb-robbery problem worked: secret entrances to the tombs, deep pits dug between the entrance and the burial chamber, or guards posted in the necropolis (cemetery). Nothing stopped the plunder of the tombs—neither long ago, nor unfortunately, today. Many thieves escaped with their stolen treasure, but some were caught. We can almost go back in time and listen in on the court trial of some of the robbers of tombs at Thebes because we have ancient Egyptian records of the proceedings of several of these trials. Just as courts today have a stenographer, or record-keeper, who writes down what happens at the trial, these papyri are the official accounts of the prosecution of ancient Egyptian thieves. Here is a confession as documented by one papyri:

> **There was brought the quarryman Amen-pa-nefer, the son of Inher-nakht. . . . He was examined by beating with the stick. . . . He said . . . "We went into the tomb of Tja-nefer, who was third priest of Amen. We opened it and we brought out his inner coffins, and we took his mummy and left it there in a corner in his tomb. We took his inner coffins to this boat, along with the rest, to the island of Amen-ipet. We set fire to them in the night. And we made away with the gold which we found on them, and four ki-te of gold fell to the lot of each man. . . ."**

As a result of some of these trials, an official committee was formed to walk through the Theban necropolis and examine the tombs, in order to see which ones had been robbed and which were still intact.

Throughout the centuries thieves stole many valuable artifacts from Egyptian tombs.

MUMMIFICATION
PRESERVING THE PAST

Have you ever dried flowers, watched grapes turn into raisins, or made pickles from cucumbers? Well, the mummification process is not so different.

The word "mummy" comes from the modern Arabic word *mumya*, meaning bitumen (a preservative). In ancient times, the Egyptians simply buried their dead in shallow graves in the desert; the hot, dry sands helped dry out the bodies and preserve them naturally. Later, in the Old Kingdom, Egyptians experimented with wrapping the body in linen bandages soaked in resin, a sticky liquid from trees. By Dynasty 4 (about 2630–2524 B.C.), the Egyptians had established the mummification technique they would use for the next 2,000 years. They did this to preserve the body for the afterlife.

The mummification process often took about thirty-five to seventy days before a body was ready for burial. First, the parts of the body most likely to decay—the lungs, liver, stomach, and intestines—were removed and placed in four containers, called canopic jars. From the Middle Kingdom (2061 B.C.) onward, the Egyptians also removed the brain (usually through the nose), which they considered unimportant because, for them, the heart was the seat of intelligence. Only the heart was left in the body.

The body was then packed with natron (a salty substance, either dry or liquid) gathered from Wadi Natrûn, west of the Nile Delta in Lower (northern) Egypt, which dried the body out and purified it. Finally, the now dried and shrunken body was wrapped in linen bandages. Paint or plaster modeling was sometimes added to restore some of the human features of the figure to the wrappings. The embalmers often placed magical amulets within the bandages for protection against evil spirits. This is one reason why robbers later attacked and ripped mummies apart, searching for gold and precious stones.

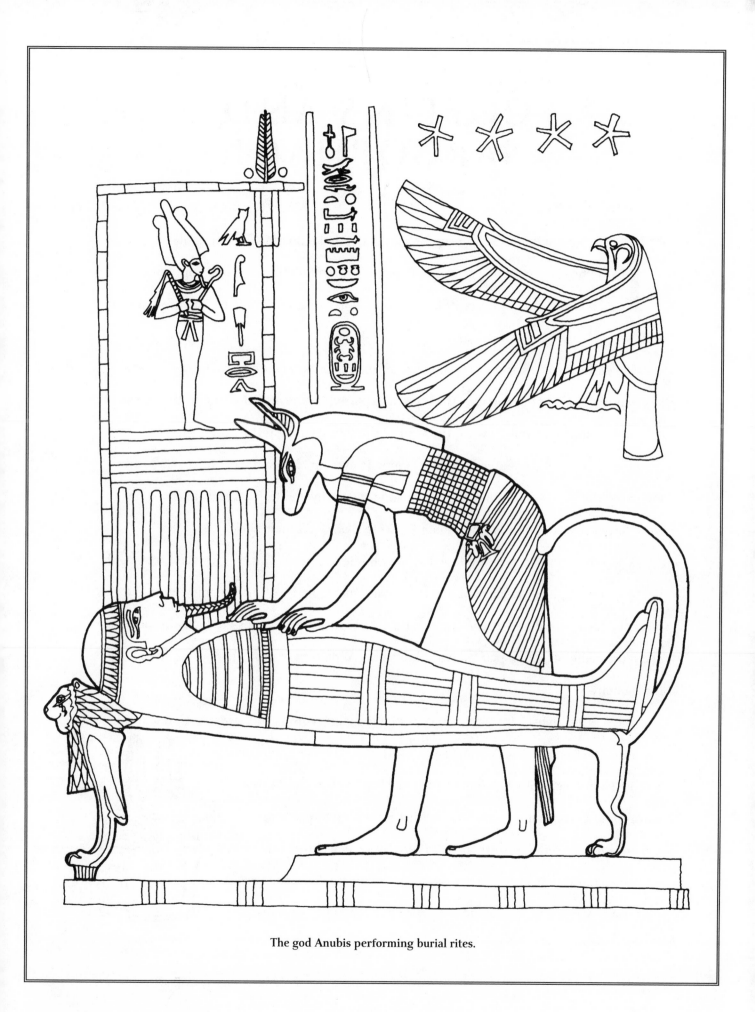

The god Anubis performing burial rites.

COFFINS AND SARCOPHAGI
BURIAL BOXES

The mummified body, ready for burial, needed a box in which it could be placed. These boxes were made of wood, limestone, granite, quartzite, and sometimes even silver and gold. Egyptologists usually use the word "coffin" for wooden boxes and "sarcophagus" for stone ones.

The earliest coffins and sarcophagi had a simple, rectangular shape; they were just large enough to hold the mummy. The body was placed inside, often leaning to the east side, so that it could "look out" toward the land of the living. To help the body "see out," the Egyptians painted or carved a pair of symbolic eyes on the outer east side of the coffin, matching the position of the mummy's head and eyes inside. Coffins and sarcophagi were larger in later periods, and mummies were placed on their backs.

A second form of coffin developed in the Middle Kingdom. This type was not rectangular, but took the shape of the human body (called an "anthropoid" coffin), complete with the head and face reproduced at one end and the feet at the other. Coffins gradually became more and more elaborate, often painted with the feathered pattern of protective wings embracing the mummy.

The fanciest, most expensive burials contained many coffins and sarcophagi, one inside the next. The tomb of King Tutankhamen (TUT-unk-AH-men), for example, revealed a mummy with a gold mask over the head, placed inside several anthropoid coffins, all of which were encased within a quartzite sarcophagus. These were surrounded in turn by several shrines. This burial was much more elaborate than the simple box or painted cartonnage—the papier maché—like wrapping—that a poor Egyptian might have had.

The mummified body of the deceased was placed within a series of decorated coffins.

BURIAL EQUIPMENT
AFTERLIFE ACCESSORIES

There were many other things that a mummy needed for a successful afterlife. Many of these items (such as special spells and texts) were originally reserved for the king only, but over the centuries, common people were allowed to have them too.

After the internal organs were removed they were placed in four separate containers called canopic jars. Each jar was protected by a different god, and often the lids of the containers were carved and painted with the head of the particular god (hawk, jackal, baboon, and human). In simple burials, the jars were undecorated limestone or pottery vessels. In elaborate burials, they were made of alabaster (calcite), faience (a hard, blue or green clay-like material made from powdered quartz, which was then glazed and fired), or other materials, with carved or painted inscriptions. Sometimes the jars were all placed within a canopic chest. In the tomb of Queen Hetep-heres [(HEH-tep-HAIR-es) the mother of Khufu, who was the builder of the Great Pyramid], which was discovered at Giza in 1925, the canopic jars contained the intact internal organs in a solution of natron that was still in liquid form after almost 5,000 years!

Egyptians believed that formulas and magical spells were also needed to guide the deceased to the next world. In the Old Kingdom, these were known as the Pyramid Texts and were offered to the king alone. In the Middle Kingdom, they evolved into the Coffin Texts and were also found written inside the wooden coffins of common people. We see them again in the New Kingdom in another form called the Book of the Dead, which was often written on papyrus and placed in the tomb for the deceased to use on their journey to the afterlife.

Canopic jars were filled with the internal organs of the deceased.

TOMB DECORATION
ART FOR THE AFTERLIFE

The mummy, the coffins and sarcophagi, and funerary spells all needed a final resting place in the necropolis. Into the tomb went the mummy of the deceased, along with burial treasure. This might include items used and cherished in life, or model objects created just for the burial that were intended to serve him or her in the next world. This is why we find Egyptian tombs filled with furniture, vessels, and containers; personal items such as combs, tweezers, sandals, and jewelry; even little models of houses, boats, workshops, and craftsmen.

The decoration of the tomb walls served a similar purpose as the items mentioned above. In the magical realm of the afterlife, painting a picture of a jar of wine or a chair on the tomb wall was just as good as actually placing the jar or chair in the burial chamber. Everything you see carved or painted on Egyptian tomb walls could, according to ancient Egyptians, magically continue to serve the deceased for all time. There were processions of offering bearers, scenes of daily life on the estate, such as fowling, fishing, craftsmanship, and sporting activities. There were hunting scenes and pictures of boat trips taken to sacred cities like Abydos (A-BY-dos) in Upper Egypt. And of course, the name(s) and administrative titles of the Egyptian(s) buried in the tomb were written all over the tomb. This helped his or her memory and spirit live on and on. Often there were biographical texts, stating what a good person the Egyptian was during his or her lifetime, such as "I gave bread to the hungry, beer to the thirsty, and clothing to the naked."

Imagine painting pictures of your favorite meal and your favorite dessert, and having them stay there ready for you whenever you wanted them—for all eternity! What would you choose?

Scenes of daily life were painted on tomb walls to serve the deceased in the afterlife.

OSIRIS AND ISIS

GODS OF THE AFTERLIFE

Many religions teach about life after death, and many of them have a particular god who rules over the kingdom in the next world. For the Egyptians, this god was Osiris (Oh-SY-ris), and he set the first example of resurrection that all Egyptians could follow. "Osiris" is actually the Greek form of the Egyptian name.

The ancient Egyptians believed that, long ago, Osiris was a king of Egypt, who reigned with his queen named Isis (EYE-sis). Osiris also had a jealous brother named Seth. One day, Seth threw a party, and during the festivities presented a box to the party-goers. He promisied to give it to whomever fit inside. When Osiris fit perfectly inside, Seth locked the box and threw it in the Nile, killing Osiris. But Isis, the queen, rescued the box, and when Seth discovered this, he dismembered Osiris's body and spread the pieces around Egypt. However, Isis and her sister, Nephthys, were able to gather all the body parts and bring Osiris back to life. Isis later gave birth to the falcon-god Horus, who avenged the murder of his father by fighting the evil Seth.

While this legend reaches back to the earliest times of ancient Egypt, Osiris first became recognized as god of the underworld in Dynasty 5 of the Old Kingdom (2524–2400 B.C.). Osiris was mainly associated with the reigning king, who lived on earth as the image of his son, the god Horus. After the king died, he became the god Osiris. Later, all Egyptians could "become" Osiris upon death. "Becoming Osiris" was the symbol for resurrection in the next world.

You can recognize pictures of Osiris because he is usually shown as a mummified figure colored white (for the linen wrappings), and with green skin because the color of plants was symbolic of rebirth and rejuvenation. He usually wears the White Crown of Upper Egypt and holds the crook and flail, symbols of royalty, as he sits in judgment over the dead. Abydos was the city where the cult of Osiris was especially sacred.

Osiris, god of the underworld, and his consort Isis.

HORUS
LORD OF THE SKIES

This falcon-headed god was identified with the ruling pharaoh on earth. Pharaoh was the "living Horus," the son of Osiris, god of the underworld.

More than any other god, Horus was protective of and identified with royalty. The titulary, or long string of names of each pharaoh, contained variations on the name of Horus, such as "Living Horus" and "Horus of Gold."

The sun and the moon were thought to be his two eyes, and the magical *udjat-eye*, or left (lunar) eye of Horus, was a popular protective amulet. Horus was often shown as a falcon or as a human with a falcon's head. In much later times, Horus appeared as a child [his Greek name was Harpocrates (Har-POC-crates), meaning "Horus the child"], often standing on and subduing crocodiles, holding snakes, and protecting people from evil spirits.

As son of Osiris, Horus was the god who avenged his father's murder at the hands of Osiris's jealous brother, Seth. Horus was also the father of four sons, who were the protective gods of the burial. They protected the internal organs that were removed during mummification and placed in the canopic jars.

Horus was worshiped all over Egypt, but cities like Hierakonpolis and Edfu (both in Upper Egypt) were especially sacred places for this god. A beautiful Late Period temple dedicated to Horus at Edfu remains to this day one of the best-preserved Egyptian temples. This temple is in the middle of the modern town of Edfu and has colossal statues of the falcon god. Since Edfu has grown up around it, the temple seems almost to have sunk partly underground in comparison to the modern buildings. You can still visit Edfu today.

The Pharaoh was the god Horus, son of Osiris.

AMEN-RE
KING OF THE GODS

Amen-Re was one of those gods whose power grew as the Egyptian empire grew. He was a composite god, a combination of two gods: Amen, whose name means "the hidden one," and Re, the traditional Egyptian sun-god.

Re was worshiped throughout Egypt during the Old Kingdom but particularly in the north. Beginning in Dynasty 4 (2630–2524 B.C.), Egyptian pharaohs called themselves "son of Re." By contrast, Amen was a god of the area of Thebes, in Upper Egypt (remember, that's south!). Although mentioned as a creator god perhaps as early as the Old Kingdom Pyramid Texts, Amen first became commonly known during the Middle Kingdom.

Amen achieved his greatest influence during the New Kingdom, when Egypt regained its independence and the foreign Hyksos [(HIK-sos) sos rhymes with close] rulers and a family of princes from Thebes began a new dynasty (Dynasty 18). Combined with Re, Amen became the most important national god of Egypt. We can see proof of this in his temple at Karnak, which each succeeding pharaoh enlarged with more columns, pylons, and courtyards. Today, the temple covers more ground than St. Peter's Cathedral in Rome. Amen-Re is most frequently called "King of the Gods, Lord of the Thrones of the Two Lands," the Two Lands being Upper and Lower Egypt. In fact, the power of this god's priesthood became so powerful that it began to challenge the pharaohs' authority in later times.

Amen-Re is usually shown in human form, wearing a crown topped by a sun disk and two plumes. Often his skin is colored blue. His most sacred animal was the ram, probably symbolic of his aspect as a fertility god. There is even a female form of this god, called Amen-et, whose statue still stands in Karnak Temple today.

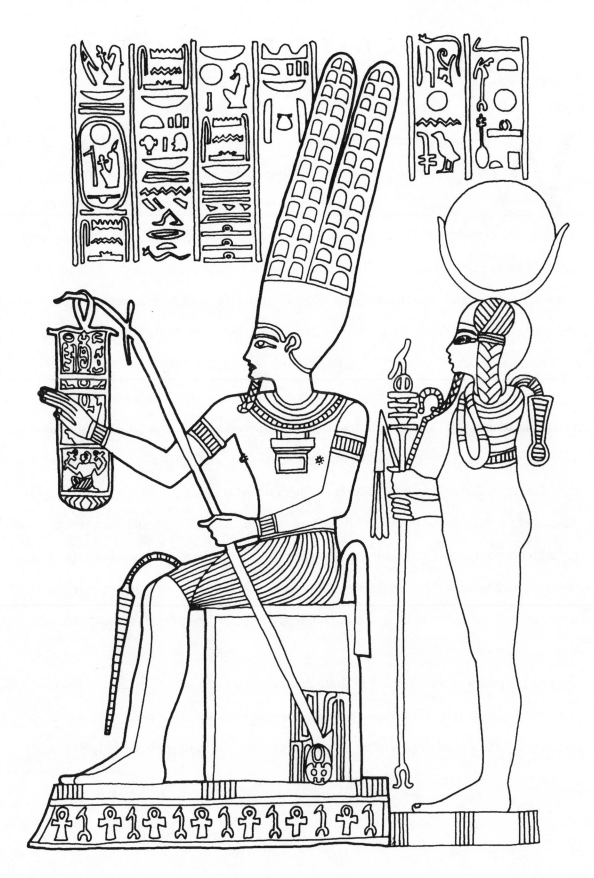

The god Amon-Re (seated), with Khonsu standing behind.

HOUSEHOLD GODS
PERSONAL PIETY

We have looked at the mighty national gods of Egypt who were associated with the king, who had huge temples dedicated to their cults, or who sat in judgment over the resurrection in the next world. But what about the everyday villagers of ancient Egypt? What gods did they worship? These men and women never caught a glimpse of the pharaoh in their lifetimes, and were not allowed into the vast and mysterious temples, nor could they read hieroglyphs. They, like the kings and queens, needed protection and guidance concerning their lives and fates as well, whether it concerned the health of a loved one or advice about the best time to sow seeds in the fields.

Alongside the great cults of Egyptian gods and goddesses, there were countless minor, or regional, deities who looked after the welfare of the common folk. In other words, there were many levels of Egyptian religion, from the state-supported festivals for the national gods like Amen-Re to the private prayers of illiterate farmers for a plentiful harvest to support their families. The comical dwarf god Bes, along with the hideous hippopotamus goddess Taweret, guarded people from evil demons while they slept. These gods watched especially over pregnant women. There were also goddesses of the harvest (such as Renenutet) and of the Nile (Hapi), who insured that neither too low nor too high a Nile would threaten lives or livelihoods.

The Egyptians made offerings to these and other similar gods. They also dedicated little statuettes or stelae (inscribed stones) to them in niches in their homes, wore protective amulets, and even purchased written appeals to the gods or to deceased relatives to help them with personal problems.

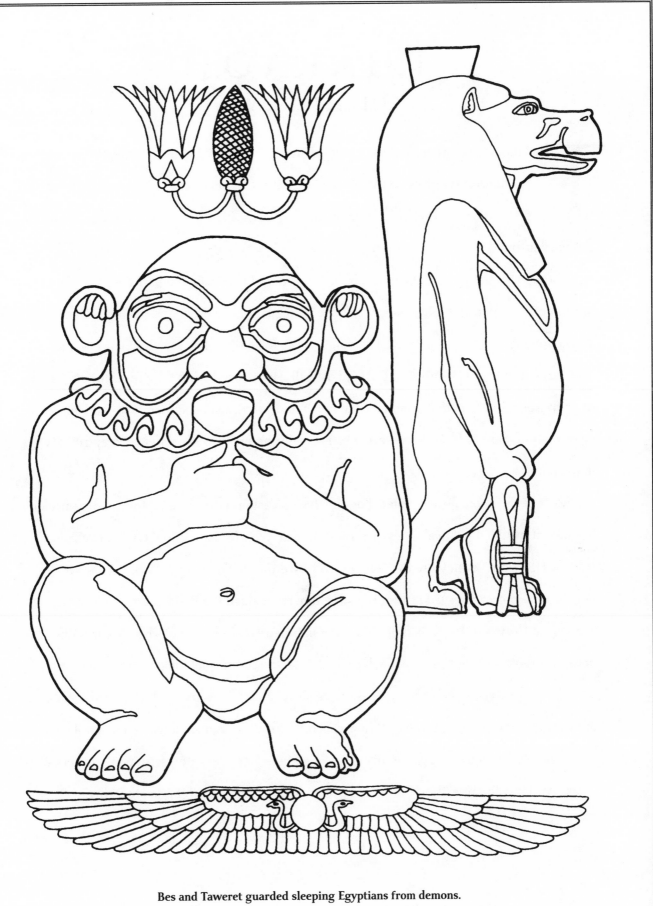

Bes and Taweret guarded sleeping Egyptians from demons.

PHARAOH
ANCIENT ROYALTY

The ancient Egyptian king was called *pharaoh*, a word that comes from Egyptian *Per-aa*, or "great house," referring to the palace. The very first pharaohs united the country around 3100 B.C. and ruled for as many as thirty dynasties, until Egypt became a Roman province in 31 B.C.

Throughout this period, the pharaoh was considered part man and part god. He was the most important person in the country, the one who guaranteed order and justice in the world, and conquered the forces of chaos. Pharaoh was the focal point between the heavens and the earth, and the chief priest in the land as well. He decided what temples to build, when to go to war against another country, what commands to make concerning taxes and legal claims, and where to build his own tomb. Typically, he married his sister to keep royalty in the family.

Most of the pharaohs were men, but on a few occasions women ruled the country, usually because of troubled political times or confusion over dynastic succession. Queen Hatshepsut (HUT-CHEP-soot) even wore the ceremonial beard that male pharaohs wore. This was not the only object reserved just for the king; others included the Red Crown of Lower Egypt, the White Crown of Upper Egypt, and the combined Double Crown. The king usually held the crook and flail (a staff and whip), and wore the ceremonial royal beard on his chin, and the cobra serpent on his brow. These were all symbols of royalty. And when you see a name in hieroglyphs written within an oval ring, called a cartouche, you are looking at a royal name.

Throughout ancient Egyptian history, some kings were very powerful while others were weak. At times the priesthood or local officials seemed just as mighty as the king.

King Tutankhamen and Queen Ankh-es-en-amen, from a decorated throne found in the king's tomb.

KING NARMER
UNIFICATION

At the very beginning of Egyptian history, there really was no "country" named Egypt. Many groups, or tribes, of people lived along the banks of the Nile River. When some of them united, others began to fight over land and water. After a time, there were two main groups, one in the north (Lower Egypt) and one in the south (Upper Egypt). It took a powerful man to unite the two halves of the country under his control. This man was King Narmer (3100–3050 B.C.); he came from the south and is thought to be the first king of the unified country of Egypt.

A famous ceremonial palette, a stone used for grinding pigments, is one of Egypt's earliest historical documents. It shows King Narmer on both sides; his figure is larger than anyone else because he was the most important person. On one side he celebrates his victory over his enemies; he holds a mace (a spiked club used as a weapon) high in one hand, ready to smite the prisoner he holds by the hair. He wears the White Crown of Upper Egypt on this side. On the other side, he wears the Red Crown of Lower Egypt.

Because Narmer lived so long ago, even long before the pyramids were built, we really don't know much about what he was like. But he must have been a powerful ruler to control a new country that was not used to such central authority. Some historians believed that Narmer is the same king as Menes, or Aha who is also found in the first dynasty of Egyptian history. Perhaps one day we will discover inscriptions of Narmer to tell us more about his life and times.

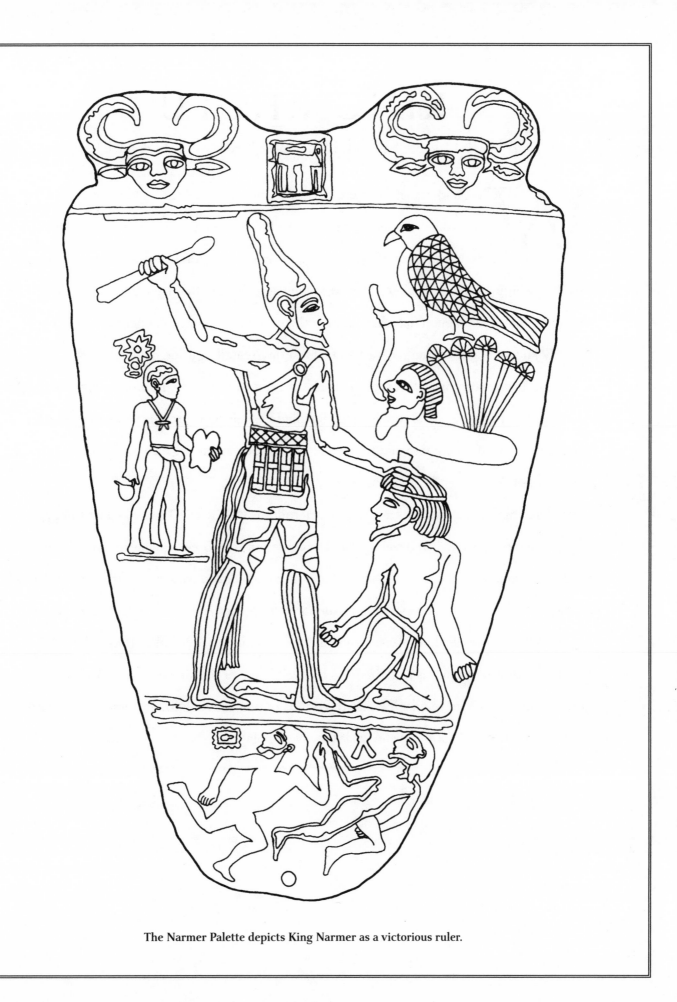

The Narmer Palette depicts King Narmer as a victorious ruler.

KING KHUFU
BUILDER OF THE GREAT PYRAMID

What kind of man built the Great Pyramid at Giza? This building was the tallest in the world for a long time; imagine the courage you would need to begin such a huge project that no one had ever dared before! Such a courageous king was King Khufu (2606–2583 B.C.). He lived so long ago, though, that we know very little else about him. Even though this pharaoh built the most impressive monument in all of Egypt, the only known statue of him (at least so far) is a tiny seated figurine made of ivory.

There is one story written on papyrus about King Khufu. He is bored and his sons entertain him with tales. One son, named Hor-djed-ef, tells of a sorcerer named Djedi, who could cut the head off a goose and then join it to its body again! He also predicted the rise of the kings who would rule after Khufu.

In later times, when Greek travelers like Herodotus (HAIR-ODD-o-tus) came to Egypt (5th century B.C.), Khufu had developed a bad reputation. The Greeks believed that he was a very cruel king who had forced slaves to build his pyramid, and who cared little for the slave's safety. But there is no ancient evidence to support such a bad reputation. In fact, it was the Egyptians themselves, and not slaves, who built the pyramid for their ruler. They believed that they would prosper from this work because the well-being of the king meant the well-being of the country. It's hard to imagine that thousands of people would build something so large and unique if they did not believe in what they were doing.

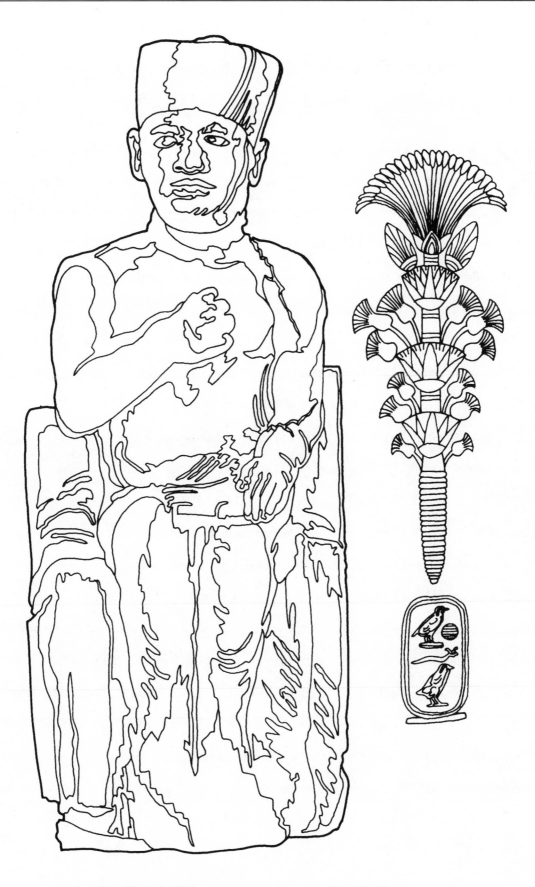

King Khufu built the most impressive pyramid in all of Egypt.

KING PEPI II
LONG-TIME RULER

King Pepi II [(PEH-pee) 2355–2261 B.C.] lived long after King Khufu, during Dynasty 6, at the end of the Old Kingdom. He lived for ninety-four years, a very long life back then—and even today! Many generations of Egyptians were born, grew up, and died knowing only this one king on the throne.

After Pepi died, the power of the kings grew very weak, and the country split apart. There were long years of economic troubles and wars. Some historians believe Pepi II was perhaps to blame because he reigned for so long and couldn't find fresh solutions to solve the country's problems. But there is also evidence of low Nile floods in the years after Pepi II, which could have exacerbated the country's problems. Also, by this time, the high officials up and down the Nile had become much more powerful and were able to challenge the authority of the king.

There is a story from happier times, before the end of the Old Kingdom, when Pepi II was a young boy on the throne of Egypt. He sent an expedition to the south, into Nubia. His commander, Har-khuf, (Har-KOOF) captured a dwarf. When Har-khuf wrote to King Pepi II recounting his adventure, the young pharaoh was so eager to see the dwarf that he wrote back: "When he goes down with you into the ship, get worthy men to be around him on deck, lest he fall into the water!" Har-khuf was so proud of this royal letter he had the text copied onto his own tomb wall at Aswan. You can still see it there today.

Pepi II built a small pyramid complex for himself at Saqqara (Suh-CAR-a). It was not as big as the pyramid of Khufu, but buried inside were Pyramid Texts, a collection of rites intended to help Pepi II through the afterlife.

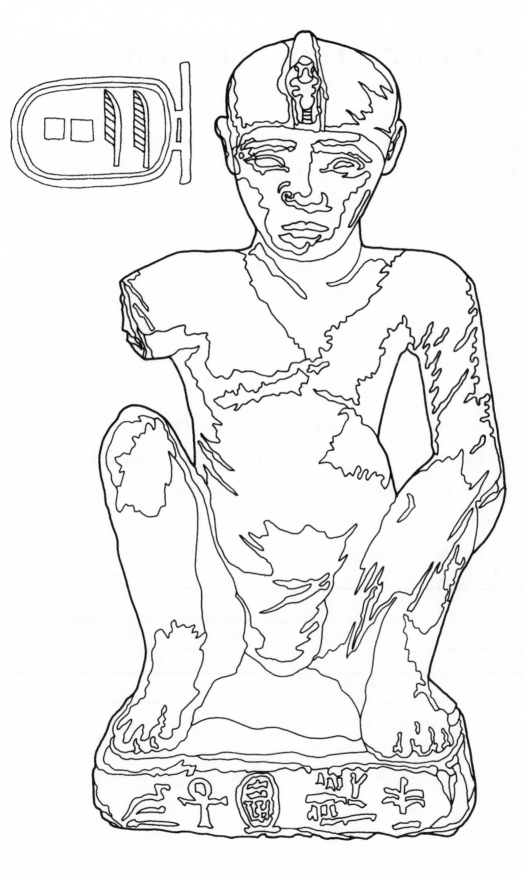

King Pepi II lived longer than any other pharaoh.

QUEEN HATSHEPSUT
KING OF EGYPT

Queen Hatshepsut (1498–1483 B.C.) was one of the most remarkable women of ancient times. During Dynasty 18, in the New Kingdom, she married her half-brother, King Thutmose II (Thut-MO-seh) and became his queen. But Thutmose died young, and his son, Thutmose III, who was borne by another minor queen, was not old enough to become pharaoh. So Hatshepsut decided to rule with him. Eventually, she took all the power for herself and became king of Egypt! She even called herself a man and some of her statues portray her with a man's chest and a ceremonial false beard of royalty.

Hatshepsut built a beautiful terraced temple at Thebes that is still one of the loveliest in Egypt. On the walls, the texts and carvings tell of her expeditions to the fabled land of Punt (on the Red Sea coast) to collect exotic plants and other objects. She also had tall obelisks (thin "shafts" of stone with pointed tops and hieroglyphic inscriptions) made and sent down the Nile by barge for the temple at Karnak. And she had a friendship with a high official named Senenmut (SEN-en-moot), whose job was to look after her daughter. Hatshepsut even built for herself a special tomb in the Valley of the Kings, which was the area usually reserved for male pharaohs.

After a reign of about twenty-six years, Hatshepsut mysteriously disappeared from history. Her young stepson, Thutmose III, by this time much older, finally took his rightful place as pharaoh and set out for battle in foreign lands.

Queen Hatshepsut is often depicted wearing the ceremonial beard of a king.

KING THUTMOSE III

WARRIOR KING

Some historians called King Thutmose III (1504–1450 B.C.) the "Napoleon" of Egypt, after the famous French general, because he fought and won so many battles and ultimately created an Egyptian empire. To judge from his mummy, he was even rather short—barely five feet tall—just like Napoleon!

At the beginning of the New Kingdom, the Egyptians had to fight to liberate their country from foreign rulers called the Hyksos. A family of warrior kings from Thebes chased the Hyksos out, and many of them kept fighting beyond the Egyptian border into Syria and Palestine. They created an Egyptian empire, and many foreign peoples had to pay taxes and tribute to Egypt. The greatest of these warrior kings was Thutmose III.

After waiting many years until his stepmother, Queen Hatshepsut died, Thutmose set out on countless military campaigns to the northeast. He also conquered parts of Nubia to the south. Thutmose III's soldiers kept diaries of the battles, and selections from these journals were carved in hieroglyphic inscriptions on the walls of the temple of Karnak and on several stelae, large inscribed stones, throughout the land.

Under Thutmose III, Egypt grew richer and more powerful; and new styles, different peoples, and languages started to change the face of the country. Pharaoh also built several temples to the gods, in celebration of his many victories. Inscriptions tell us that Thutmose knew his hieroglyphs well, he collected different types of plants on his travels, and designed vessels. He died at the age of fifty-three, and his mummy is in the Cairo Museum.

Thutmose III set out on countless military campaigns, and was one of Egypt's greatest warrior kings.

KING AMEN-HOTEP II
ATHLETIC RULER

King Amen-hotep II [(AH-men-HO-tep) 1453–1419 B.C.] continued the military campaigns of his father, Thutmose III, during the 18TH Dynasty. This king was very proud of his athletic ability. Often royal inscriptions exaggerate wonderful things about the king. We call this royal propaganda. But Amen-hotep's hieroglyphic texts mention so many different sports in his inscriptions that there is probably some truth to his claims.

After he became king, Amen-hotep II ordered a stela, or large flat stone, inscribed and set up near the Pyramids of Giza in a special temple to the Sphinx. This stela tells us all about Amen-hotep's athletic skills. It reads:

> Now, when he was still a youth, he loved his horses and rejoiced in them. He was determined to work them, to learn their nature, to be skilled in training them and understand their ways. . . .When it was heard in the palace by his father . . . his majesty's heart was glad to hear it. . . . Then his Majesty said to those beside him: "Let him be given extremely fine horses from my Majesty's stable which is in Memphis. . . ."

The Sphinx stela of Amen-hotep II also describes how the king could handle the stroke oar in a boat of 200 oarsmen and not get tired, even though the others had "become weak, their limbs limp. . . ." Amen-hotep could also shoot an arrow through a copper target from a racing chariot so that it came out the other side! This was "a deed which had never been done before nor heard of by report. . . ."

Amen-hotep's mummy was one of the very few to be discovered still in its original coffin in his tomb in the Valley of the Kings.

Amen-hotep II was said to possess the strength of many men.

KING THUTMOSE IV
SPHINX DREAM STELA

Another pharaoh of Dynasty 18 was Thutmose IV (1419–1386 B.C.). One day, when he was a young prince, and his father Amen-hotep II, was pharaoh, Thutmose IV went hunting near the Pyramids of Giza. At midday, young Thutmose got off his chariot and took a nap in the shadow of the Great Sphinx, which was then covered with sand up to its neck, for it was over 1,000 years old. Remember, the pyramids by this time were ancient monuments. The prince dreamt that the sphinx appeared to him, and said "Look at me, my son Thutmose . . . I am your father, who will give you my kingdom on earth at the head of the living . . . You must be as my protector, for my condition is as if I were ill in all my limbs. The sand of this desert upon which I am, has reached me. . . ."

The Sphinx promised to make the young prince pharaoh if only he would dig away the sands that covered his great body. Thutmose did this and years later became pharaoh.

How do we know about this story? Thutmose decided to have it written in a long hieroglyphic inscription upon a stone stela and placed between the Sphinx's paws at Giza. It still stands there today, and when you learn to read hieroglyphs, you can go there and read the story for yourself!

Thutmose IV slept by the Sphinx and dreamed of greatness.

KING AKHENATEN
ONE GOD

When Egyptologists look back over thousands of years, it is often very hard to learn much about the personality of some ancient Egyptians because their writings are formal, religious, or political. Rarely do we learn what a king or queen or a poor farmer by the Nile, really thought and felt.

One example is King Akhenaten [(AH-Ken-AH-ten) 1350–1334 B.C.], who lived and ruled with his wife, Queen Nefertiti (Nef-err-TEE-tee), in Dynasty 18 during the New Kingdom. Akhenaten broke with many Egyptian traditions because he was interested in one god in particular called the Aten. It represented the light of the sun's disk. He told his followers to scratch out the names of the old gods in tombs and temples all over Egypt. He even decided to leave the capital city of Thebes and build a brand new capital called Akhet-aten ("City of the Horizon of the Aten") many miles to the north. He was not interested in the military campaigns of the kings before him; instead he wrote religious hymns to the Aten. He created an entirely new art style so that humans were shown with very long features, long necks, thick thighs, and egg-shaped heads. This new style must have come directly from Akhenaten, for no artist would have dared to show people this way without royal permission.

Unfortunately for Akhenaten, his revolution failed after about twenty-five years and his religious and artistic innovations were dropped entirely after his death. The new king, Akhenaten's son-in-law Tutankhamen, (TUT-unk-AH-men) returned to Thebes and to the old gods. However, many of Akhenaten's changes in art and language have survived over the years.

King Akhenaten was a revolutionary in Egyptian religion and art.

KING RAMESSES II
PHENOMENAL PHARAOH

King Ramesses II [(RA-mes-ease) 1279–1212 B.C.] is better known as Ramesses the Great. He lived during the 19TH Dynasty of the New Kingdom, and for more than sixty-five years he controlled the country, fought Egypt's enemies, built hundreds of temples, and had more than fifty sons! He is also the only Egyptian pharaoh to visit Paris; his mummy was sent there from the Cairo Museum in the 1980s because it had to be treated and conserved.

Ramesses II fought an important battle in his fifth year as king against the Hittites. It was called the Battle of Kadesh. In his twenty-first year, Ramesses signed a peace treaty with the Hittites and inscribed a copy of it on temple walls. He built huge temples at Thebes, where his Hypostyle Hall in the temple of Karnak looks like a huge forest of stone trees, covered with thousands of painted hieroglyphs. On the other side of the Nile, he built a funerary temple for himself; in 1817, over 3,000 years later, a large fallen head from one of his colossal statues inspired the poem *Ozymandias* by English poet Percy Bysse Shelley ["My name is Ozymandias (OH-zee-MAN-dee-us), king of kings; Look on my works ye mighty and despair!"].

Farther to the south, at Abu Simbel, in Nubia, Ramesses built two temples carved inside the solid rock of the cliffs. One temple shows four colossal statues of Ramesses seated and facing the sun, while the other has statues of his favorite queen, Nofretari (NO-fret-TAR-ee). Her tomb in the Valley of the Queens is one of the most beautiful to survive; its delicate wall paintings were recently restored by an international team of conservators.

In the late 1980s, perhaps the largest tomb ever built in Egypt was found in the Valley of the Kings. Known as KV5, it is still being excavated today, and it may hold the burials of many of Ramesses' fifty sons. Some people hope that this tomb may bring us new evidence about Ramesses's role in the Biblical Exodus, when the Hebrews were thought to leave Egypt under Moses's leadership.

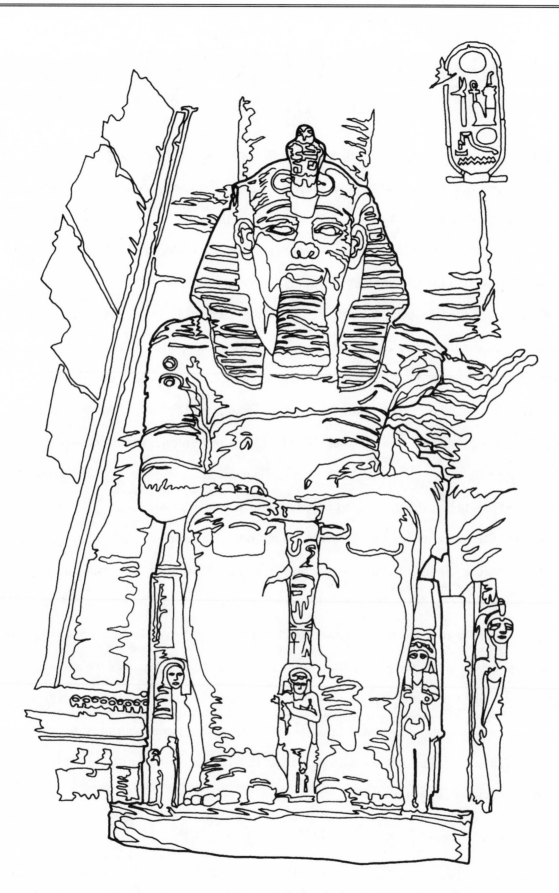

Ramesses II ruled more than sixty-five years and had about fifty sons.

QUEEN CLEOPATRA
QUEEN OF QUEENS

At the very end of ancient Egyptian history—before modern history begins—one famous woman, Cleopatra, lived a fascinating life. The Cleopatra we know best was actually Cleopatra VII (69–30 B.C.). Egypt, at this time, was ruled by the Ptolemies, a dynasty originally of Macedonian rulers descended from one of Alexander the Great's generals. The power of Rome was very strong in the Mediterranean.

After gaining the Egyptian throne in the year 51 B.C. Cleopatra met Julius Caesar and bore him a son four years later. After Caesar was killed, Cleopatra met and married Mark Antony, who granted her territory in Phoenicia and Cilicia and proclaimed her "queen of queens." This angered the rest of the Romans, who fought and defeated Antony and Cleopatra at the Battle of Actium in 30 B.C. Shortly thereafter, Antony committed suicide, and on August 12, 30 B.C. Cleopatra did the same. She allowed a poisonous asp (Egyptian cobra snake) to bite her. When she died Egypt became a Roman province.

Perhaps Cleopatra was not so different from Queen Hatshepsut, back in Dynasty 18. Both women were intelligent, both wanted power, and both had great accomplishments on the throne of Egypt. But in Hatshepsut's time, Egypt was in control of its own destiny, and the Mediterranean world must have seemed less crowded. Under Cleopatra, many different cultures, especially Rome, were competing for control of the region. Much of the ancient Egyptian language and culture had disappeared from contact with foreigners; most of the country spoke Greek, and only devoted priests in the Egyptian temples continued to practice the ancient rituals and hieroglyphs with expertise. Hatshepsut would probably not have recognized Egypt in Cleopatra's time.

Cleopatra's politics caused a war, and upon her death Egypt became a Roman province.

IMHOTEP
THE ARCHITECT

Every country has its geniuses, brilliant writers, talented artists, worthy leaders, and gifted thinkers. One of the earliest such men known to us is Imhotep. He was the architect for the Step Pyramid complex for King Djoser [(JOE-zer) 2687–2667]. While King Djoser certainly gave the order to build the Step Pyramid, it was most likely Imhotep, his architect, who conceived and designed the project. We will talk later about the famous Step Pyramid complex built for King Djoser at Saqqara from Dynasty 3 (see page 98), It is probably the world's earliest monumental building in stone. It is also possible that Imhotep was responsible for organizing all the workers to get the job done on time, too.

We do not know much about Imhotep's (Im-HO-tep) personality, but we do know he was involved in the Step Pyramid construction. His name is mentioned on the base of a statue of King Djoser that was discovered in the complex. Later generations of Egyptians worshipped him as a legendary figure, and by Dynasty 26 (660–525 B.C.) he had been named a god!

Many statuettes of Imhotep are known. He is usually shown seated on a stool, studying a papyrus unrolled upon his lap. He became symbolic of wisdom, writing, and medicine, and had his own temple and priesthood at the ancient Egyptian city of Memphis. Perhaps his tomb will one day be discovered at Saqqara, not far from the Step Pyramid itself.

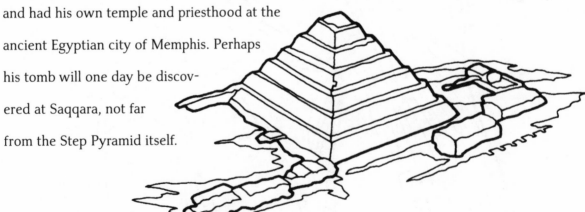

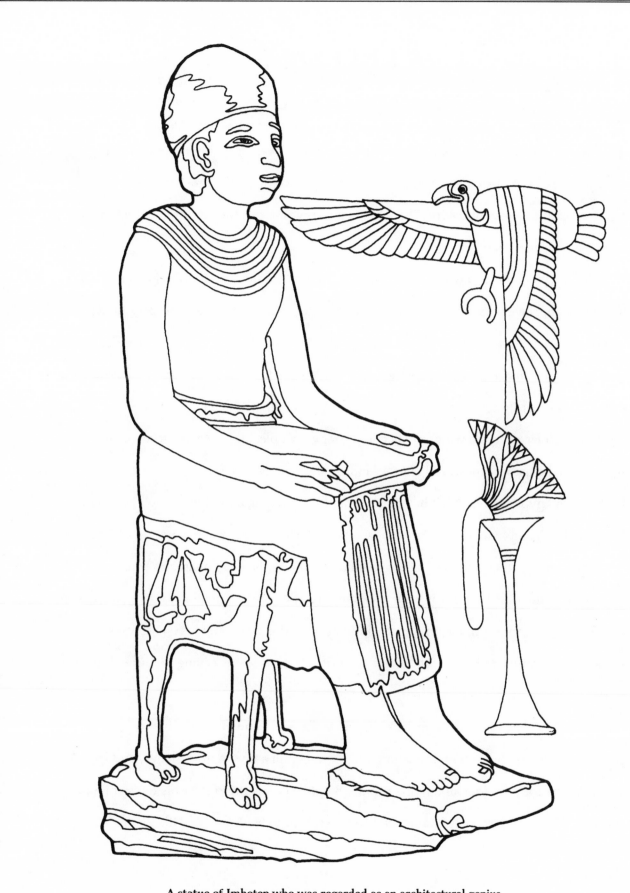

A statue of Imhotep who was regarded as an architectural genius.

SINUHE
THE HERO

Sinuhe, whose name means "son of the sycamore," was probably not a real person, but the hero in an ancient Egyptian classic tale, perhaps the most famous story in all of Egyptian literature. There are many copies of this tale, written on both papyri and flakes of limestone.

The story begins during the 12TH Dyansty (in the Middle Kingdom), when an official, named Sinuhe, hears that King Amenemhet I (1991–1962 B.C) is dead. Sinuhe flees to Syria in a panic. Some Egyptologists believe that the king was murdered and Sinuhe fled out of guilt and fear of punishment, but the story is not clear. Perhaps he was just afraid. The hieroglyphs tell us: "My heart fluttered, my arms spread out. A trembling befell all my limbs."

Sinuhe travels far and wide, meets many strange people, and observes foreign customs. In Palestine he battles a powerful warrior and emerges victorious. But he begins to miss his home in Egypt and fears that he might die and be buried in a foreign land without a proper Egyptian tomb and funeral. (The Egyptians believed this was one of the worst things that could happen.) At this point a royal command comes from the dead pharaoh's son and successor, Senwosret I (Sen-wos-ret), also known as Sesostris. Sinuhe is forgiven for fleeing and will be welcome at home, in Egypt. Upon hearing this news, the hero is so excited that he decides to return to Egypt right away. He writes the new king, saying he did not mean to flee from Egypt, but was overcome with dread.

Upon returning to Pharaoh's palace, Sinuhe faints while bowing down before Senwosret I. But there is no cause for fear; the young king grants him a new house, riches, and even preparations for a wonderful Egyptian tomb. Sinuhe spends the rest of his days enjoying the king's favor and never feels the need to flee from the banks of the Nile again.

Sinuhe kneels before the Pharaoh.

KHA-EM-WASET
THE ARCHAEOLOGIST

We like to think that archaeology is a "new" field of study, one that is less than one hundred-fifty years old. But, would you believe that there was an ancient Egyptian—a prince, no less—who might have been one of the world's first archaeologists?

Kha-em-waset (Ka-em-WA-set), the fourth son of King Ramesses II (1279–1212 B.C.), was born in his father's first year on the throne in Dynasty 19 and died in his father's fifty-fifth year. In addition to being the high priest of Memphis, Kha-em-waset built several temples there and at other sites. He also expanded the Serapeum, the burial place of the sacred Apis bulls at Saqqara. His tomb, which has yet to be located, may be at Saqqara near the Serapeum.

Kha-em-waset also spent much time excavating and restoring the pyramids of many pharaohs of the distant past, reinscribing their names and ensuring that their memories would live on. These archaeological activities later brought him the reputation of a magician!

Stories from Egypt's Ptolemaic and Roman Periods (332 B.C.–A.D.395), long after Kha-em-waset's death, turn him into a fictional character in grim tales of the living versus the dead. But Kha-em-waset was surely one of Egypt's most learned men, who had a deep respect for the long history of his country and its monuments. Modern Egyptians now think like Kha-em-waset as they try to preserve and protect their ancient sites for the world to study and enjoy.

Workers restoring an ancient pyramid.

SAQQARA
SACRED CEMETERY

Where would you find the very first example of monumental architecture in stone? At Saqqara. This sacred necropolis (cemetery), or city of the dead, located at the edge of the western desert (southwest of modern Cairo) has a long history.

In the very first Egyptian dynasties (3100–2705 B.C.), large mudbrick tombs were built here, with complex niches and paneling around their edges that Egyptologists call "palace facade" after the houses and palaces they resembled. Saqqara became especially famous when King Djoser (2687–2667 B.C.) of the 3rd Dynasty decided to build a huge tomb complex here in stone. Djoser took the concept of the mastaba tomb and stacked one mastaba on top of another until he had built a step pyramid with multiple tombs. In addition, the complex had an enclosure wall, courtyards, ceremonial palaces, columns resembling papyrus plants, and shrines. But many of these are merely dummy buildings, with doors that lead nowhere or rooms only hinted at; much of Djoser's Step Pyramid complex seems to have more of a magical, ritual meaning than any practical purpose.

Saqqara has other pyramid complexes too, many of which were built after Djoser's Step Pyramid. Several belong to the high officials of the Old Kingdom, some of them with as many as forty decorated chambers. And more are being discovered all the time. In recent years, an entire necropolis of New Kingdom tombs, quarried deep underground in the limestone cliffs, has come to light. There are many lifetimes of work for Egyptologists here.

One of the most unusual burial places in all of Egypt is the Serapeum at Saqqara. This is a series of connected underground caverns, housing the gigantic stone sarcophagi of the sacred Apis bulls buried here from the New Kingdom through the Late Period. If you think a cemetery of sacred bulls is unusual, other areas at Saqqara hold hundreds of sacred jackal and ibis burials, each sacred to particular Egyptian gods. Saqqara has many secrets yet to tell.

An Apis bull found at Saqqara.

GIZA
AWESOME SIGHTS

If Saqqara produced the first monumental stone building (the Step Pyramid), Giza produced the most famous archaeological site in the world. By the time of Dynasty 4 (2630–2524 B.C.), the Egyptians were building true pyramids (not step pyramids) out of thousands of limestone blocks, and three kings of that dynasty—Khufu, Khafre, and Menkaure (Men-cow-RAY)—chose Giza as the site for their funerary complexes.

Giza lies just west of Cairo (and north of Saqqara), on a plateau overlooking the Nile floodplain. Here Pharaoh Khufu built the Great Pyramid; Pharaoh Khafre built the second pyramid; and Pharaoh Menkaure built the third pyramid. But there is much more to this necropolis than these three artificial mountains. There are ritual pyramids (one of which was just discovered at the southeastern corner of the Great Pyramid in 1991), the Great Sphinx of Khafre, and hundreds of civilian mastaba tombs surrounding the large pyramids.

This site is the first example of a necropolis laid out and developed according to a well-organized plan, with row upon row and street after street of mastaba tombs, with decorated chapels, statues, and burial shafts cut deep underground. The thousands of hieroglyphic inscriptions on tomb walls here tell us much about the government.

In recent years, archaeologists focused much of their attention on protecting this site from overcrowded tourism and urban development. They are also exploring new areas to see how the builders of the pyramids lived. Ancient bakeries and fish-processing buildings have turned up, as well as new tombs belonging to the foremen who oversaw the construction of the pyramids. Some of the human skeletal remains even show evidence of stress from years of lifting heavy stones.

Giza was so impressive that even ancient Egyptians visited in later dynasties. The Great Pyramid at Giza continues to amaze visitors today. It is the only surviving wonder of the seven wonders of the ancient world.

Tourists travel to Giza.

AMARNA
AKHENATEN'S VISION

This site, located on the east bank of the Nile, is a very unusual one. It does not have thousands of years of history, as do Abydos or Memphis, but was built on the order of a single New Kingdom pharaoh, King Akhenaten (1350–1334 B.C.).

Akhenaten focused all of Egyptian religion on the sun disk, known as the Aten, and moved the court to Akhet-aten, modern Tell el-Amarna. Akhet-aten means "City of the Horizon of the Aten." Imagine having to build the town or city where you live in just a few years! Much of the work was very hasty, but many people moved here with the king. There were houses, temples, palaces, workshops, and even tombs constructed in the nearby cliffs. Most of the city was abandoned after Akhenaten's death, and now it is the archaeologists who "live" there. The British and Germans spent many years excavating the city, its temples, and the tombs, both royal and private ones.

It is at this site that the famous head of Queen Nefertiti was found, along with many other statues of the king and queen and some of their daughters. Many of these pieces are now in the Cairo Museum and in a museum in Berlin, Germany. From the ruins of the buildings, foundation walls, and floors, archaeologists can reconstruct much of the original appearance of the ancient city.

Each year scientists uncover more about this fascinating period of Dynasty 18, when one king deeply affected Egyptian history.

This bust of Queen Nefertiti was found at Amarna.

THEBES

VALLEYS OF THE KINGS AND QUEENS

One of the most important Egyptian cities was Thebes, called "the city of a hundred gates." Although probably just a small town during the Old Kingdom, Thebes grew in importance twice, when two different Theban families reunited the country to start the Middle Kingdom (2061–1784 B.C.) and the New Kingdom (1570–1293 B.C.).

Today, when people travel several hundred miles south of Cairo to Upper Egypt, they see the modern town of Luxor surrounding the ruins of Thebes, one of the greatest capital cities of the ancient world. Vast temples, settlement areas, and hundreds of tombs cover both the east and west banks of the Nile. On the east bank, the major monuments are the New Kingdom temples of Karnak and Luxor, huge complexes that once had armies of workers.

On the other side of the Nile was the land of burial for thousands of Thebans, including many kings and queens. At the beginning of Dynasty 18, the Egyptian pharaohs chose a hidden valley for their final resting places. It began a tradition of impressive royal tombs cut into the Theban cliffs, snaking underground from chamber to chamber. This region, known as the Valley of the Kings, has been the sight of some of the most amazing archaeological discoveries ever made: the tombs of King Tutankhamen, of Thutmose III (1504–1450 B.C.) and Seti I (1291–1279 B.C.). Tomb KV 5, whose true size and significance was discovered in 1995, possibly holds the burials of some of the fifty sons of Ramesses II of Dynasty 19 (1279–1212 B.C.). Just to the south is the preserved village of Deir el-Medineh, where the craftsmen who built and decorated the royal tombs lived together.

The west bank at Thebes also has the Valley of the Queens, containing some of the loveliest tombs of all. The painted tomb of Queen Nofretari, wife of Ramesses II, still shows colors as bright and fresh as when they were painted more than three thousand years ago. Like so many Egyptian monuments, this tomb's paintings are very fragile but were recently conserved by an international team of specialists.

A wall painting in the tomb of Queen Nofretari.

ABU SIMBEL
TWO TEMPLES

This site is famous for two temples carved right out of the sandstone cliffs at the edge of the Nile's west bank by the order of King Ramesses II (1279–1212 B.C.). Located far to the south, in ancient Nubia, these two temples have facades with colossal statues of the king and his queen, Nofretari, which must have impressed both Egyptians and Nubians alike with the awesome power of pharaoh. The larger temple shows four enormous seated figures of Ramesses II, with a smaller, standing statue of Re-Horakhty [(RAY-Hor-AK-tee) a form of the sun god] carved into the cliff face between them. One can actually walk between the four figures of Ramesses into the temple, where more colossal statues of the king serve as pillars. In the inner sanctuary of the temple sit four life-size statues together—Re-Horakhty, Ptah (P-TAH), Amen-Re, and Ramesses himself. Twice a year, the sun's light penetrates all the way into the temple to illuminate these four figures.

The smaller temple at Abu Simbel is dedicated to the goddess Hathor (a protection goddess). Colossal statues of Queen Nofretari, dressed as the goddess Hathor, appear on the facade between still more figures of Ramesses II. The decoration of the interior of this temple is similar to Ramesses's own temple, except that the innermost sanctuary shows the goddess Hathor as a sacred cow emerging from the mountain.

When the powerful Aswan High Dam was built, it threatened to drown these two temples in the lake it created, now called the Nubian Sea. So, between 1966 and 1968, both temples were carved up into thousands of small pieces, moved to higher ground and reconstructed piece by piece. Today they remain one of the most popular sites in all of Egypt, an amazing achievement of *both* ancient times and modern times.

Colossal statues of the mighty Ramesses and his queen, Nofretari, at Abu Simbel.

ABYDOS
HOLY CITY

One of the oldest and holiest sites, Abydos is located in Upper (that is, southern) Egypt on the west bank of the Nile. Here the rulers of the earliest dynasties were buried in a series of pits and tombs far out in the desert. It is difficult to know what these tombs looked like, for only the portions below ground survived. Closer to the floodplain was one of the oldest temples, dedicated to Osiris, god of the underworld and the resurrection. There are monumental mudbrick structures here from as early as Dynasty 2; in recent years these have revealed a series of ancient wooden boats buried all around them. Many boats still await excavation.

Perhaps the most impressive monument at Abydos is the temple begun in the New Kingdom by Seti I (1291–1279 B.C.) of Dynasty 19 and completed by his son, Ramesses II (1279–1212 B.C.). This limestone temple contains some of the finest relief sculpture carving in all of Egypt, and many of the figures and hieroglyphs still show their original color, even after 3,000 years. In one of the chambers of this temple, the Egyptians carved a king list, or list of all the pharaohs up to Seti and Ramesses, along with figures of Seti and Ramesses making offerings to the pharaohs. This is a very important document for the history of Egyptian kingship, and it also shows us what the Egyptians thought about their own history, because some kings they included and others they left out.

Abydos remained a holy pilgrimage site throughout Egyptian history. Many Egyptians came here and commissioned stelae (monuments) in honor of Osiris to be set up as permanent mementos or offered prayers. In tomb walls all over Egypt, there is often a scene of the tomb owner traveling in his boat to the sacred city of Abydos.

King Seti I receives the gift of life from the god Thoth at Abydos.

THE TOMB OF QUEEN HETEP-HERES

SECRETS IN THE SAND

In 1925, members of the Harvard University-Museum of Fine Arts, Boston Expedition were working at the famous site of Giza, as they had year in and year out since 1905. Just to the east of the Great Pyramid, one of the photographers noticed that the leg of his camera tripod sank into the ground in an unusual way. Upon further examination, the excavators realized it was a hidden shaft over one hundred feet deep. At the bottom was a tomb that had been sealed for more than four thousand years. In one corner they could see a large stone sarcophagus, and surrounding it were thousands of fragments of pottery vessels, stone and copper dishes and vases, wooden furniture, scattered inlays and bits of gold leaf.

It took the archaeologists nearly two years to clear out the room. Because of their methodical and scientific approach, they were able to reconstruct the ancient gilded and inlaid furniture placed in the tomb, and they even identified the tomb's owner from the gold hieroglyphs on the tomb floor. The name read Hetep-heres, who was the wife of King Snefru (2630–2606 B.C.) and mother of King Khufu (2606–2583 B.C.). The expedition had discovered the tomb of the mother of the builder of the Great Pyramid, so far the only partially intact royal burial from the Old Kingdom ever to be found. The whole excavation project took 280 days, required 1,057 photographs, and filled 1,701 pages of notebook records.

After the tomb was finally cleared, it was time to open the sarcophagus. To the excavators' surprise, it was found to be empty! It was hard for the excavators to imagine this burial taking place, if there was no mummy of the queen. One theory is that perhaps the body of the queen was robbed at the time of her burial.

An elaborate carving on the bed canopy of Queen Hetep-heres

THE PYRAMID BUILDERS
SETTLEMENTS IN SOUTH GIZA

For centuries visitors to the site of Giza have wondered how the pyramids were built. In recent years we have begun to answer this question better than ever before. Egyptologists have located the quarries of most of the core stones for the pyramids, they've identified traces of mudbrick ramps used for hauling the blocks up the pyramid, and have begun to excavate the settlements and tombs of the pyramid builders themselves.

To the south of the Giza Pyramids is a massive enclosure wall with a gateway. On the southern side of this wall lies a recently discovered settlement area that archaeologists believe housed the huge work force needed to construct the royal pyramids. So far, an ancient bakery, brewery, and a fish-processing house have been identified. A short distance away lie the modest tombs of some of the workers here. They range from simple mudbrick burial shafts for the poorest workers, to limestone mastaba tombs with carved inscriptions farther up the hillside. These fancier tombs probably belonged to the foremen in charge of the construction project. Many of the skeletons found show traces of severe back problems, probably from moving heavy stones.

We do not have all the information about this area yet, but additional excavations have much to tell us. We hope to learn how the work gangs were organized, who was in charge of what projects, how they were housed and fed, and perhaps even who did the laundry! These discoveries will help us appreciate the pyramids as a very human achievement, one that all Egyptians, royal and common, rich and poor, participated in and were proud of.

Some Egyptians developed severe back problems from moving and lifting heavy stones for the pyramids.

THE MODELS OF MEKET-RE
ANCIENT RELICS

In Dynasty 11, around 2000 B.C., an official named Meket-re (Meket-RAY) built a tomb for himself hidden high up in the cliffs on the west bank at Thebes. Meket-re chose to include with his burial treasure, twenty-five painted wooden models showing all the aspects of life on his estate. These were magical objects that, like painted scenes on tomb walls, were supposed to magically come alive to serve him in the afterlife. There were offering bearers, fishing boats, processions of cattle and herdsmen, weavers' and carpenters' workshops, a slaughterhouse, and pleasure yachts. While the burial of wooden models became a fairly common practice in the Middle Kingdom, most models were crude, with stick figures and simple details. But Meket-re's models were all carved and painted by master craftsmen; each one shows us a glimpse into the daily life of the ancient Egyptians.

Four thousand years after the models were sealed in the tomb, excavators from New York's Metropolitan Museum of Art discovered the chamber. On March 17, 1920, when the Egyptologist Herbert Winlock aimed his flashlight through a hole in the tomb wall, this is what he wrote:

> "... a little world of four thousand years ago, and I was gazing down into the midst of a myriad of brightly painted little men going this way and that. A tall, slender girl gazed across at me perfectly composed; a gang of little men with sticks in their upraised hands drove spotted oxen; rowers tugged at their oars on a fleet of boats ... And all of this busy going and coming was in uncanny silence, as though the distance back over the forty centuries I looked across was too great for even an echo to reach my ears."

Today, these models are on display at both the Egyptian Museum, Cairo, and the Metropolitan Museum of Art, New York.

Models of workers and animals were found in the tomb of Meket-Re.

THE TOMB OF TUTANKHAMEN

"EVERYWHERE THE GLINT OF GOLD"

Two years after the discovery of Meket-re's models, and three years before Queen Hetep-heres's burial shaft at Giza was uncovered, Egyptologist Howard Carter (1874–1939) was excavating in the Valley of the Kings at Thebes on behalf of Lord Carnarvon (1866–1923). Carter had so far found little there after many years of work, and 1922 was to be his last excavation season. But on November 4, 1922, just a few days after he returned to the site, the first step of a carved staircase leading downward was unearthed. The excavators cleared the staircase, removed debris from a long corridor, and stood at last before a sealed door to Tutankhamen's tomb. When Carter put his eye up to a hole pierced through the wall, all he could see was gold. "Everywhere the glint of gold," he is quoted as saying. The antechamber he saw contained ceremonial couches in the shape of animals, boxes of linen, chariots, and life-size statues. Three more chambers remained to be discovered behind this one: the burial chamber, the treasury, and an annex. Tutankhamen's tomb remains the only royal one discovered almost intact. This was because workmen's huts were built right over the tomb, hiding it for thousands of years from potential robbers.

Even though he died in his late teens, Tutankhamen lived in a very interesting period at the end of Dynasty 18 (1334–1325 B.C.). The "experiment" in the new religion of Akhenaten (focusing on the god Aten) had just ended, and Tutankhamen was the pharaoh (or more likely, it was the older priests and advisors around him) who returned things to "normal," with religion restoring prominence to the Theban god Amen.

In modern times, "King Tut," as he is now known, has become the most famous pharaoh throughout the world. And, despite the rumors of a curse on the discoverers of the tomb, Carter lived to a ripe old age. Today, Egyptologists are still studying thousands of objects from the king's tomb.

King Tutankhamen's innermost coffin was made of solid gold.

ROYAL MUMMIES
HIDDEN BURIALS

The great pharaohs of the New Kingdom left their mark all over Egypt. Great temples, military campaigns, stone statues, royal decrees, and even foreign marriages and treaties are all part of New Kingdom history. But because most of the royal tombs in the Valley of the Kings were robbed centuries ago, no one in modern times ever expected to see the actual mummies of these famous kings. Imagine the amazement about one hundred years ago, when a secret burial place—the hiding place of the great ones of ancient Egypt—was discovered.

Tomb robbing had become so common by the later periods of Egyptian history that the pious priests of Dynasty 21 (1070–946 B.C.) realized they had to gather the royal mummies out of their plundered tombs and hide them from further damage. One of their hiding places was found in 1881—a secret tomb south of the terraced temple of Queen Hatshepsut at Deir el-Bahari. At the bottom of a deep shaft and long passage was a burial chamber containing forty coffins with the mummies of some of the greatest rulers of Dynasties 17 to 20, among them Kings Amenhotep I, Thutmose I-III, Seti I, and Ramesses I and II.

Legend has it that when these great rulers were sent by boat down the Nile to the Egyptian Museum in Cairo, the villagers all along the river mourned these kings from three thousand years ago. In 1898, more mummies were found hidden in the tomb of King Amenhotep II, including those of Thutmose IV, Amenhotep III, Merenptah, Seti II, and Ramesses IV–VI. Many of the mummies have been X-rayed and examined, in the hope that we might learn more of the family histories, health, and diet of these ancient rulers. They are treated with care and respect today in a special room in the Egyptian Museum in Cairo.

Citizens observe the ship carrying the discovered mummies.

TOMB KV 5

BURIAL OF FIFTY SONS

There were many people who excavated in the Valley of the Kings and then said they believed the valley was exhausted. But this was even before the discovery of the tomb of Tutankhamen! If we have learned one thing, it is that the Valley of the Kings continues to surprise us. Many Egyptologists have spent years walking back and forth over ground that *later* produced wonderful treasures.

Recently, yet another surprise shocked the world: the discovery of tomb KV ("King's Valley") 5, perhaps the largest and most unusual royal tomb ever built in Egypt. Although it will take years to excavate this tomb properly, it seems to be the burial place of fifty sons of King Ramesses II (1279–1212 B.C.), known as Ramesses the Great.

American Egyptologist Kent Weeks examined this area of the Valley in recent years because the Egyptian antiquities authorities planned to widen the road and create a turnaround for the many tour buses visiting the area. Tomb KV 5 had already been explored as early as 1825, but no one had penetrated very far into it; it looked like just another unfinished chamber filled with debris. But when Weeks cleared part of this chamber in 1995, he discovered beyond it a vast pillared hall, a long corridor with a statue of the god Osiris at the back, and many chambers leading off to the right and left of the corridor. Mysterious staircases not yet explored lead downward to still more chambers, and perhaps it is here that Ramesses's sons might be buried. Most of the chambers have to be cleared of debris that reaches almost to the ceiling (due to flash floods and drifting mud and sand) before archeologists will know what treasures await us in KV 5. We have much to learn about the history of Dynasty 19, an age of international politics, battles, and treaties, and this large family of pharaohs certainly played an important role. There are more discoveries to come.

A statue of the god Osiris was found at the end of a passage in KV5.

LUXOR TEMPLE
PIT OF STATUES

In ancient Egypt, one way to worship the gods and seek their favor was to dedicate a statue to them in a temple. Kings and high officials often commissioned such statues placed in chambers throughout the temple. After many generations, some temples became choked with too many statues; something had to be done to make more room. But they could not simply be destroyed. So sometimes a pit was dug, and the statues were gathered together and buried; a sort of a temple housecleaning. The ancient Egyptians had no idea how exciting it would be for us in modern times to discover such a pit full of statues. One of these was found in 1903-4 in Karnak Temple and contained 800 statues and stelae, along with 17,000 smaller objects. A smaller, but equally exciting, cache turned up recently in Luxor Temple at Thebes in 1989.

Egyptian archaeologists were testing the soil for dampness inside the court of King Amenhotep III (1386–1349 B.C.) in Luxor Temple on January 22, 1989, when a slab of finely smoothed stone turned up. This turned out to be just the beginning of the discovery: up came a perfectly preserved, inscribed, standing statue of Amenhotep III, then seated statues of the goddesses Hathor and Iunyt, a kneeling figure of King Horemheb (1321–1293 B.C.) presenting offerings to the god Atum, an alabaster sphinx of King Tutankhamen, a Horus falcon, a gigantic cobra, and many more. In all, twenty-six statues were found, buried one under the next, stretching many meters underground. Judging from the very late styles of pottery and other objects found in the pit, the statues were probably buried in Roman times (around A.D. 400), when parts of Luxor Temple were converted into a Roman camp. Today the statues are on display not far from the temple, in the Luxor Museum of Ancient Egyptian Art.

Luxor Temple.

DIGGING, RECORDING, TRANSLATING, PRESERVING
LEARNING FROM THE PAST

Egyptology today is a very exciting field; there are so many different ways to make a contribution to our knowledge of the past. You can use not only what you know about the ancient Egyptians, but also many different skills you might have learned from other studies, such as drawing, photography, surveying, speaking foreign languages, working with computers, and public speaking.

One of the main occupations of the Egyptologist is archaeology. The goal is to excavate ancient sites (houses, towns, tombs, temples, palaces) methodically and responsibly, keeping careful records of all the finds, their locations, and their condition. The archaeologist spends just as much time writing up notes, taking pictures, and making reports, as he or she does digging. This way, others can share in the discovery and help to interpret it, even if they were not at the site at the time of the dig.

All of the recorded information must be studied and processed. Architectural features must be drawn and planned, organic materials, such as plant remains, must be analyzed, texts must be translated, and pottery and other objects restored, photographed, and drawn. This work helps us to "rebuild" on paper the ancient site and to bring us one step closer to understanding the ancient Egyptians. But we cannot stop there because many sites are in danger of being lost forever, due to changes in climate, and urban development. (In 1995, the spectacular tomb KV 5 was discovered at the entrance to the Valley of the Kings, where plans almost went ahead to build a concrete tourist bus turnaround.) Egyptologists must try to preserve, restore and protect these fragile monuments, so that future generations will be able to marvel at the ancient Egyptians just as we do today.

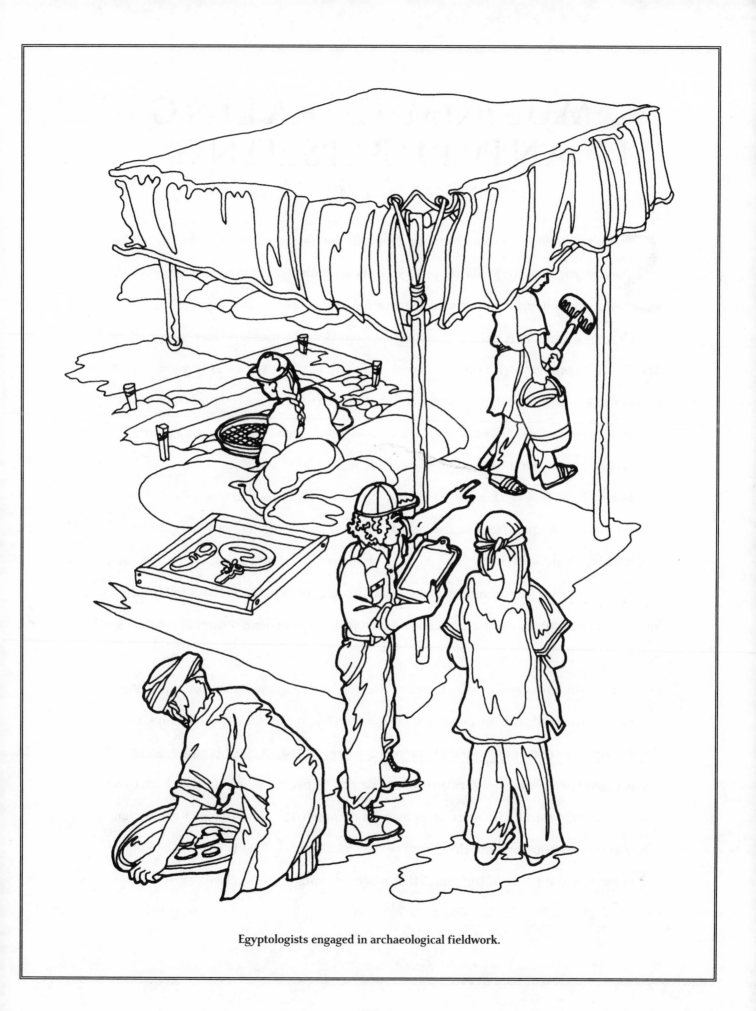

Egyptologists engaged in archaeological fieldwork.

MUSEUM CURATING
AND PUBLISHING
ANCIENT EGYPT TODAY

Some Egyptologists do fieldwork in Egypt during part of the year. Others teach history, art, hieroglyphs, or archaeology in schools and universities. And still others work as curators in museums around the world with Egyptian collections.

What is a curator? A curator cares for the objects in the museum, making sure they are displayed properly, with the right label information. He or she gives lectures to museum visitors, assists visiting scholars who want to study particular objects, organizes special exhibitions (sometimes traveling with priceless statues around the world as a courier), and writes articles and books about the collection.

In fact, publishing is a big part of Egyptology. There are thousands of books about every subject you can imagine, from ancient bread- and beer-making along the Nile, to studies of hieroglyphic personal names and pictures of ancient Egyptian turtles. From such books, you can learn how to write your name in Demotic, or a tomb painting dates to Dynasty 1 instead of Dynasty 30, and how to create an ancient Egyptian love potion or create a spell against cockroaches.

Publishing books and articles is one of the best ways Egyptologists communicate with each other and with anyone else who is interested in the subject. Nowadays, many Egyptologists use computers to draw hieroglyphs, reconstruct ruined temples, and send ideas electronically to colleagues around the world. As people share ideas and discoveries, each generation learns a bit more and passes that knowledge on to the next generation. The Egyptians themselves did this for more than 3,000 years. That is part of the human experience, and it is one of the things that makes learning fun. Don't you agree?

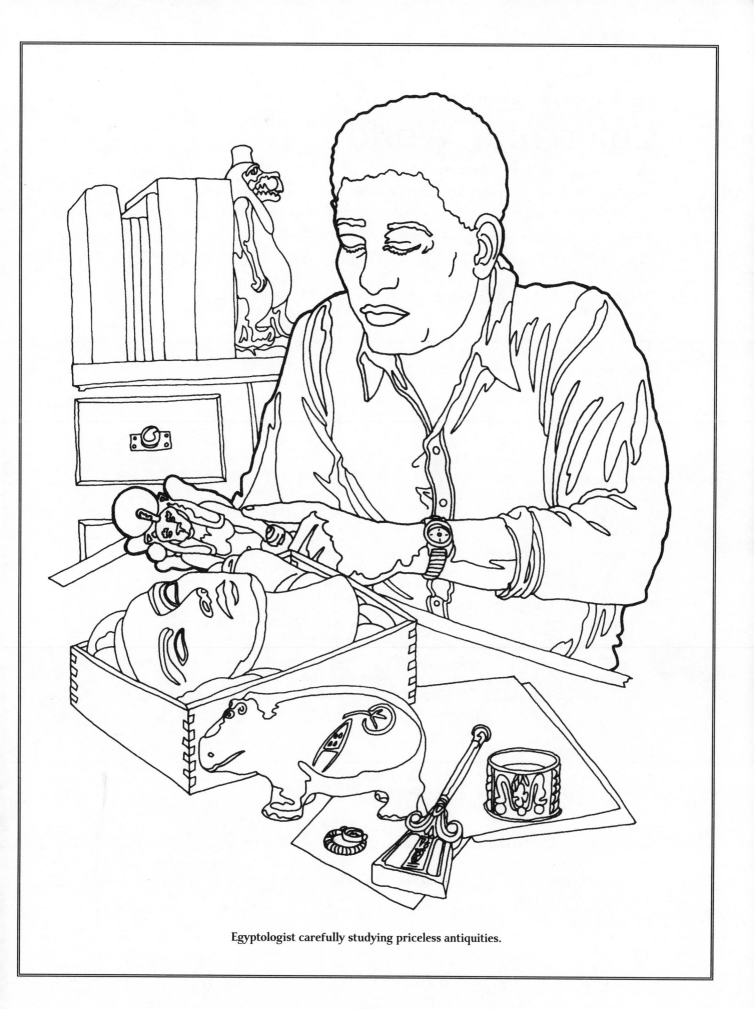

Egyptologist carefully studying priceless antiquities.

THE RUNNING PRESS START EXPLORING™ SERIES

Color Your World

With crayons, markers, and imagination, you can re-create works of art and discover the worlds of science, nature, and literature. Each book is $8.95 and is available from your local bookstore. If your bookstore does not have the volume you want, ask your bookseller to order it for you (or send a check/money order for the cost of each book plus $2.50 postage and handling to Running Press).

THE AGE OF DINOSAURS
by Donald F. Glut

Discover new theories about dinosaurs and learn how paleontologists work in this fascinating expedition to a time when reptiles ruled the land.

THE AMERICAN WEST
by Emmanuel M. Kramer

Explore the lives and legends of the American West—with 60 images to color.

ARCHITECTURE
by Peter Dobrin

Tour 60 world-famous buildings around the globe and learn their stories.

AUDUBON'S BIRDS OF AMERICA
by George S. Glenn, Jr.

Read about the adventures of naturalist and artist John James Audubon, and let your imagination soar with this field trip to the fantastic world of American birds.

BALLET
by Trudy Garfunkel

Brilliant choreographers and dance companies-from the classic elegance of Noverre to the modern moves of Jerome Robbins and Twyla Tharp.

BULFINCH'S MYTHOLOGY
Retold by Steven Zorn

An excellent introduction to classical literature, with 16 tales of adventure.

FOLKTALES OF NATIVE AMERICANS
Retold by David Borgenicht

Traditional myths, tales, and legends from more than 12 Native American peoples.

FORESTS
by Elizabeth Corning Dudley, Ph.D.

Winner, Parents' Choice "Learning and Doing Award"
The first ecological coloring book, written by a respected botanist.

GRAY'S ANATOMY
by Fred Stark, Ph.D.

Winner, Parents' Choice "Learning and Doing Award"
A voyage of discovery through the human body, based on the classic work.

NATURAL WONDERS
by Bettina Dudley

Visit wild places and meet amazing creatures—60 breathtaking sights in all.

OCEANS
by Diane M. Tyler and James C. Tyler, Ph.D.

Winner, Parents' Choice "Learning and Doing Award"
An exploration of the life-giving seas, in expert text and 60 pictures.

PLACES OF MYSTERY
by Emmanuel M. Kramer

An adventurous tour of the most mysterious places on Earth, with more than 50 stops along the way.